Topics
in
Applied
Linguistics

Topics in Applied Linguistics

Ronald Wardhaugh
The University of Michigan

NEWBURY HOUSE PUBLISHERS, INC./rowley, massachusetts

NEWBURY HOUSE PUBLISHERS, INC.

 Language Science
Language Teaching
Language Learning

68 Middle Road, Rowley, Massachusetts 01969

ISBN:

Paper: 912066-79-2
Cloth: 912066-10-5

Printed in the U.S.A.   First printing: March, 1974
                                                    Second printing: February, 1975

Preface

This book has its genesis in a number of articles published over a span of half a dozen years. These articles have focused mainly on the teaching of reading and the teaching of English as a second language, but other topics have been treated from time to time. No attempt has been made to eliminate every redundancy in rewriting previously published articles for inclusion as chapters here, for some redundancy is a necessary part of any linguistic expression. However, excessive repetition has been avoided and coherence has been sought. Hopefully, the result is what is claimed for it—a treatment of various topics in applied linguistics rather than a definitive work on applied linguistics. The latter is an impossible task. A much more modest goal has been set, and the reader is left to judge how successfully it has been achieved.

Thanks must be expressed to the Research Club in Language Learning, The National Council of Teachers of English, Teachers of English to Speakers of Other Languages, and the International Reading Association for permission to base many of the chapters on previously published articles. Readers will also recognize that the first and ninth chapters cover some of the same ground as parts of two earlier published books: *Introduction to Linguistics* (McGraw-Hill, 1972) and *Reading: A Linguistic Perspective* (Harcourt, Brace and World, 1969). Thanks of a different kind are due to the many secretaries who typed different versions of articles and this manuscript, and to colleagues for criticisms and suggestions. And very special thanks are due to my family for their forbearance when the various duties of recent years have prevented me from spending as much time with them as we would all have liked.

CONTENTS

part one

Language and Linguistics

chapter one
Language

Apparently language has always fascinated men, for many stories exist about its origins, how it changes, and what powers it can have over people. Within society language both divides and unites and within almost every educational system it holds a preeminent position. However, at the same time language is a little understood phenomenon even though much has been said and written about it. Therefore, it may be useful to begin by saying a few things about language from the perspective of linguistics, the scientific study of language.

A DEFINITION

One way of approaching a phenomenon to be studied is to attempt a definition of that phenomenon so as to exclude extraneous matters from consideration. For this reason linguists have sometimes defined language as a system of arbitrary vocal symbols used for human communication. There are problems with such a definition in that its usefulness depends on adequate definitions of the key terms, and agreement is not always possible over such definitions. However, an attempt is worthwhile so that some broad principles can be stated at the outset.

The principal term in the definition is *system*. Language must be systematic, for otherwise people could not learn a language nor could a language be used consistently. A speaker of a language uses only certain sounds and combinations of sounds. An English speaker can say *Don't do it now* but he cannot say *Dntdtnooiow* or *Ndtoionwtod*. Every language actually has two systems, one of sounds and the other of meanings. Linguists try to describe the characteristics of the two systems and how the systems relate to each other within one total linguistic system for the particular language as a whole. The nature of this relationship in all languages is very important and constitutes a most interesting problem, for it is in this respect that languages apparently share certain very important universal characteristics.

A related issue concerns the kind of phenomena that the linguist must cover and how he is to obtain that coverage. One kind of coverage would consist of a catalog of observations of linguistic phenomena according to a simple scheme of classification. For example, a dictionary is such a catalog of observations about words and their meanings. However, it is quite impossible to compile a dictionary of the sentences of a language in the same way that a dictionary of the words of a language can be compiled. Whereas the supply of words in a language is finite their possible combinations in sentences are infinite. Consequently, ways must be sought for describing sentences and parts of sentences and sounds and combinations of sounds in a way that says something of interest about the systematic nature of language.

An appreciation of the kinds of difficulties that can occur may be gained by asking what kind of system is required to account at the same time for the multiple negation of *I don't have none neither*, the ambiguities of *They have mended socks*, and the apparent structural similarities of *Fred is certain to please, Fred is eager to please*, and *Fred is easy to please*. We could ignore dialects in which multiple negation is normal, refrain from resolving sentence ambiguity, and concern ourselves with a single level of syntactic structure. In fact, many linguists have spent a lifetime in linguistics without ever having concerned themselves with such problems. However, today we must insist that all these sentences contain phenomena that must be accounted for within a single theory which provides some means for discussing these apparently unrelated phenomena.

Linguists are also concerned with deciding what the best set of units and processes is for describing languages. Utterances are not continuous phenomena: they consist of discrete units of various sizes arranged by various processes. Linguists seek to understand what these units and processes are. It is very likely that they are not those that the educated public holds dear, certainly as these are defined by that public, for example such units as letters and words and such processes as sentences constructed according to certain sense-making formulas. Instead they are such units as phonemes and morphemes, and such arrangements and processes as constituent structures and transformations. The linguists' search is for those discrete units and processes which systematically account for interesting data within a theory that says something of importance about language.

The term *arbitrary* does not mean that everything in a strange language is unpredictable, for languages do not vary in every possible way. It means rather that it is impossible to predict exactly which features will be found in a particular language if it is completely unfamiliar. There will be no way of predicting what a word means just from the way it sounds, no way of knowing whether or how nouns will be inflected, and no way of saying what patterns of concord and agreement will exist. Likewise, there will be no way of predicting exactly which sounds will occur, of knowing what clustering possibilities will exist, or of saying that there will be both oral and nasal vowels. However, if languages were completely unpredictable in their systems, the terms *noun, cluster,* and *vowel* would be of no use. Linguistic systems are not completely unpredictable, for languages do resemble each other in many important ways.

Deletion, that is the permissible omission of a part of a sentence when that part can be predicted from what remains, is a good example of a nonarbitrary language characteristic. The process may be illustrated in English using the following deletions: *We could have won and they could have won too; We could have won and they could have too;* and *We could have won and they too.* Such a deletion process will be found in all languages, but the particular form it takes will depend on the language. Likewise, all languages will have processes for negation, as in the negation of the *We ate* to *We didn't eat.* In this English example, the positive sentence is negated by the insertion of *n't,* the introduction of the verb *do,* and the assignment of the "past tense" from the verb *eat* to the verb *do.* This English negation process is rather complicated. It is possible to imagine much simpler processes as the example *We ate* negated to **We ate we ate* or **We ate ate we* or **We ate ate,* that is through some system of total sentence repetition or total or partial inversion. But such possibilities never occur in natural languages. Language is unpredictable only in the sense that the variations of the processes that are employed are unpredictable. Certain very simple logical processes are never employed, as in the above ungrammatical examples of negation, but certain seemingly illogical and obviously complicated processes are preferred, as in English negation.

The term *vocal* refers to the fact that language is primarily speech and it is speech for all languages regardless of the state of development of their writing systems. The continued existence of preliterate societies, the knowledge we have of language acquisition by children, and the existence of historical records all confirm that writing is based on speaking. Writing systems exist primarily to capture sounds and/or meanings on paper, and the primary purpose of writing is to lend some kind of permanence to the spoken language.

Since speech is primary, any thorough study of language must be concerned with phonetics and phonology. All this is not to deny the importance of writing and writing systems and the possible effects of mass literacy on language systems and linguistic usage. It is undeniable that writing influences speaking. The insistence on the primary speech is an insistence on the importance of the historical primacy of speech over writing and a denial of the common belief that speech is a spoken, and generally somewhat debased, form of writing.

The term *symbol* refers to the fact that only a minimal connection exists between the sounds that people use and the objects to which these sounds refer. Language is a symbolic system in which words are associated with objects, ideas, and actions by convention. In only a few cases does some direct connection exist between a word and some phenomenon in the real world. Onomatopoetic words like *clang, crack*, and *sigh* are examples from English, but the meanings of these words would not be at all obvious to speakers of either Chinese or Eskimo.

The term *human* refers to the fact that the kind of system that interests us is possessed only by human beings and is very different from the communication systems possessed by other forms of life. Just how different, of course, is a question of some interest, for it can shed light on language to know in what ways human languages are different from systems of nonhuman communication. We may ascribe the differences to the process of evolution that man has gone through and say that they result from the genetic characteristics that distinguish man from other species. No system of animal communication makes use of concurrent systems of sound and meanings, and few systems of animal communication use discrete arbitrary signals. Moreover, none allows its users to do all that language allows human beings to do: reminisce over the past, speculate about the future, tell lies at will, and devise theories and a metalanguage about the system itself. Bees do not discuss last year's supply of food, dolphins are not next-year oriented, jackdaws do not deceive each other with their calls, and dogs do not bark about barking.

The final term *communication* refers to the fact that language allows people to say things to each other and express their communicative needs. Language is the cement of society, allowing people to live, work, and play together, to tell *the* truth but also to tell *a* lie, or lies. Sometimes it is used merely to keep communication channels open so that if any need arises to say something of importance a suitable channel is available. This last function is met through the conventions of greeting and leave-taking, by small talk, and in idle chatter. Language also functions to communicate general attitudes toward life and others and to bind together various kinds of social groups.

LINGUISTIC THEORY

The definition of language which has just been given still allows for a wide range of possible inquiries. One kind of inquiry would involve no more then making a set of observations of one kind or another. A second kind of inquiry might demand that such observations be made according to a certain set of principles. For example, we might argue that it is not enough to say that so many people of such and such a social or regional background use sentences like *He sad* and *He asked could he eat* and make no attempt to relate these sentences to other sentences from the same speakers, such as *He be sad* and to the almost certain nonappearance of a sentence such as *He asked if he could eat*. A decision as to what constitute the data which must be described and the principles that must be observed in the description will therefore control what we have to say. The decision effectively controls the actual selection of the data. If the linguist feels he must describe certain kinds of relationships, he will look for examples of such relationships and for additional evidence. On the other hand, if he is not aware of these same relationships, he will fail to notice certain phenomena.

Some kind of system is necessary for organizing the data, because science is concerned with the development of systems for handling data and with theory building. The most appropriate system for describing a language will share all the characteristics of any good scientific theory. It will be an abstraction in that it will make reference to idealized units and processes. However, at the same time it will acknowledge that these idealizations are realized in various ways in the real world, just as the physicist's gravitational system and the economist's monetary system are abstractions realized respectively in falling bodies and price fluctuations. The system will attempt to relate apparently diverse phenomena within a single theoretical framework, will provide a terminology for making observations about such phenomena, and will stimulate interesting investigations. A system must do all these things if it is to be scientific and useful.

A system can show relationships among apparently unrelated phenomena. Sentences like *John kissed Mary* and *The boy chased the dog* can be related to each other as exhibiting the same *pattern*; words like *Mary* and *dog* can be considered to be *nouns*; *Mary was kissed by John* and *The dog was chased by the boy* can be regarded as *transformations* of the first two sentences, and both **John Mary kissed* and **The boy dog chased* can be regarded as *ungrammatical*, and therefore starred, because either they do not apparently occur in real life or they violate certain *rules* which speakers of the language apparently follow. In these examples the diverse phenomena are related through a set of terms.

This set should not be *ad hoc*, devised for a particular language; rather it should be a set that can be used to describe phenomena in any language. It is for this reason that attempts have sometimes been made to describe all languages within a particular terminology. For example, attempts have sometimes been made to describe English as though every word must belong to one of eight parts of speech or in terms of phonemes or morphemes which can be discovered by following a prescribed set of procedures, or through possibilities and impossibilities of occurrence, for example the possibility of *Be quiet!* but the apparent impossibility of **Be tall!*

Each set of terms arises from a theory and together the theory and terminology require an investigator to look at a language in a certain way. The investigator does not merely fit data into a theoretical framework using the available terminology to do so; rather, that framework helps him to delineate just what are the data and questions with which he must be concerned. Consequently, at various times certain questions about language have been held to be answerable, but at other times not. A good theory also leads to the formulation of interesting questions so that gaps in a conceptual framework may be explored and new linguistic evidence used to confirm or deny basic hypotheses.

Linguistics is a science only insofar as linguists adopt scientific attitudes toward language. Scientific attitudes require objectivity. The investigator must not deliberately distort or ignore data but must try to see things clearly and see them whole, all the while admitting that his theoretical inclinations influence his view of the data. Moreover, these theoretical inclinations should be quite uninfluenced by the scientist's emotions. A scientific statement must also be verifiable, and the techniques and experiments on which it is based must be replicable, since explicitness is an essential requirement of the scientific method. A scientist must also be thorough in his treatment of problems and reject arbitrary solutions. However, often different competing theories exist at any one time, each claiming adequacy in covering what purport to be the same data. The result may be vigorous conflict among supporters of the various theories, and developments in a discipline may appear to be revolutionary rather than evolutionary. Such has been the case in linguistics in the last twenty years.

A PAIR OF DISTINCTIONS

Before going any further we should look at a pair of distinctions that linguists find it useful to make. One is a distinction between *descriptive linguistics* and *prescriptive linguistics* and the other a distinction between *competence* and *performance*. The former distinction is implicit in all linguistic writing and the latter is often quite explicit.

The description-prescription distinction relates to the fact that linguists try to avoid making prejudicial judgments about data. A sentence such as *I don't have none neither* is to be explained not criticized. Such sentences occur and must be accounted for. They may well produce undesirable consequences when uttered in certain circumstances, but this observation is social not linguistic in nature. To say the *I don't have none neither* is a *bad* sentence is to make a prescriptive statement about behavior not a descriptive statement about language. Nor is it an ungrammatical sentence for the speaker and for the listener. It can be compared with a collection of words such as **Have don't I none*. A linguist must describe the occurrence of the former and account for it in some way within a general linguistic theory. In addition, he may try to account for the nonoccurrence of the other group of words; however, not everyone would agree that this second task is a proper linguistic task. On no account though, can a linguist dismiss *I don't have none neither* as either incorrect or of no linguistic interest merely because such an expression is in low social repute.

The competence-performance distinction relates to the fact that the linguist's system should account for a native speaker's knowledge of his language as well as the actual linguistic forms that he uses. This knowledge allows the speaker to understand and produce utterances which he may never find the opportunity either to understand or to produce. This ability to understand novel sentences derives from the speaker's competence. This same competence causes him to reject ungrammatical sentences, tells him which sentences are ambiguous, and indicates to him when other speakers have become sidetracked in the middle of sentences. Actual linguistic performance is full of utterances which get sidetracked or are interrupted in various ways. Many linguists consider that the most fruitful linguistic approach is not to describe such utterances, but to describe the underlying system, or competence, which leads a speaker-listener to produce-understand them.

At the same time the underlying system should allow the linguist to give some account of ambiguous sentences and to show where ungrammatical sentences fail. Actual utterances will not, however, be ignored, but neither will they limit the scope of linguistic inquiry. Furthermore, the judgments and intuitions of native speakers about their language may be consulted. Almost universal agreement exists that any grammar which treats well-formed sentences in a language on the same basis as disconnected utterances is missing more than one important generalization about that language in particular and language in general.

CONCLUSION

Language is uniquely human. Languages also appear to share some universal constraints. We can assume that these contraints exist because of human limitations or predispositions. Children apparently learn languages in the same way no matter how different the cultures in which they are raised. Such universal learning is of interest to both psychologists and linguists. Language is also probably the most creative system possessed by man. Psychologists and linguists, therefore, have an interest in linguistic phenomena, the former to explain behavior in general, the latter to explain linguistic behavior in particular.

Finally, although languages are learned, they must also occasionally be taught, or there must be some teaching about linguistic matters. Linguists can be expected to contribute some understanding of language to this teaching. They may also sometimes offer advice about the substance of what must be taught, and say how it should be taught. When such statements are made with a full understanding of the complex processes of teaching and learning, they should be listened to with attention. However, too often they are not made with such an understanding, for linguists are just as prone as any other professionals to offer gratuitous advice in areas outside their realm of competence. Nor are linguists always completely objective in their own use of language. But such is to be expected. Language is heady stuff and not even the most self-disciplined linguist can entirely resist being influenced now and again by some of its more mysterious properties nor avoid being trapped occasionally during his own linguistic performance.

chapter two
The Relevance of Linguistics

Fundamental disagreements continue to exist among those responsible for curricula in the public schools about the teaching of grammar. In colleges and universities, too, controversy may develop over the place of grammar or, more broadly characterized, linguistics in departments oriented by tradition toward the study of literature. Such controversy may arise over the nature of linguistic inquiry itself or over the extent to which any future generations of college English professors and school teachers should be familiarized with linguistic developments. Since such controversy exists and is likely to continue to exist into the forseeable future, it may be appropriate to examine certain specific issues that are involved in making decisions about the teaching of grammar and about the various possible ways of teaching grammar. Such an examination seems particularly necessary in view of recent developments in linguistics itself.

LANGUAGE STUDY

At the outset we must say that no valid objection can exist to the study of grammar, of English or of any other language, in colleges and universities. Languages exist, they are systematic, and these systems and linguistic theory itself, therefore, have as much claim to be worthy of study as have solar, chemical, and social systems and any other kind of scientific theory. In colleges and universities the main problems are not those of the justification of language study, but rather problems of staffing and tradition.

The staffing patterns and traditional interests of academic departments often cause problems when new areas of knowledge begin to open. For example, there is good reason for the majority of English professors to feel uncomfortable in the presence of a linguist and even on occasion to be overtly hostile to his discipline. The reason may be found in their training. English departments, like many departments bearing "language" names, are almost without exception departments devoted to the study of literature—English literature, French literature, German literature, and so on—and not departments devoted to the study of both literature and language. As a result of their training, English professors, the products of such department, are likely to feel far more comfortable discussing the poetic works of Chaucer, Shakespeare, and Browning than discussing the linguistic works of Chomsky, Sapir, and Bloomfield. A movement to introduce a "new" English into the classrooms of the public schools is therefore unlikely to be initiated at a meeting of the English department chairmen of our colleges and universities. A "new" English will not take over like the "new" mathematics as a result of a healthy push from academia. It is even unlikely that chairmen will be able to pursue the much more modest goal of broadening the linguistic offerings of their departments, as some undoubtedly would like to, for they are going to be much too busy for years to come just keeping their departments afloat on the seas of ever-increasing enrollments and generally shrinking job markets and budgets to spare energy for anything so potentially divisive to their existing faculties as increasing the required linguistic content of English programs to any great extent.

The fact is though that many courses in the grammar of Modern English are even now taught on college and university campuses. They are taught by linguists and others in miscellaneous departments which may or may not be departments of English or Linguistics. Usually such courses are taken by linguistics majors, a rather small group at even a major linguistic center, by graduate students in various linguistic concentrations and by majors in education. On many campuses it is often this last group that constitutes the majority in classes on English grammar and students from English departments are likely to be conspicuous by their absence. It seems strange that the most basic of all humanistic studies, the study of one's own language, could be so sadly and generally neglected by those who often claim to be the most well-rounded in their preparation to teach humanities. One can only wonder at times how it is possible to discuss English literature, particularly poetic literature, without a rigorous training in English phonology and syntax. Still experience indicates that it is done, in fact that such is the norm, with the sad result that what sometimes passes for profound literary insight is no more than profound linguistic ignorance. Furthermore, the present system with its seemingly deliberate scorning of linguists and linguistic knowledge does nothing to guarantee intelligent criticism of such a basic piece of work as a new dictionary or book on usage, and, in fact, as was shown by the controversy a few years ago over *Webster's Third New International Dictionary*, seems to guarantee just the opposite.

The fact that education majors often occupy many of the seats in English grammar classes apparently indicates that some educators insist that future teachers, particularly high school English teachers, become aware of the structure of the language that they will teach during their professional careers, even though at the moment the curriculum guides used in schools almost never advocate formal teaching about that language. Most such guides condemn the teaching of traditional grammar because educators point to studies which show that such teaching has no carry-over to composition. Furthermore, the study of grammar for its own sake finds few defenders in the public schools. There is good reason to suspect, however, that much traditional grammar still continues to be taught because almost all the undergraduates and teachers who take introductory courses in linguistics readily define adjectives as words which modify or describe nouns, nouns as naming words, and so on through the whole apparatus of traditional school grammar. In the light of such evidence and of other reported studies of what goes on in English classrooms, it seems fair to say that many teachers still fall back on traditional grammar to fill some of the class time in English either in attempts to alter types of disapproved linguistic behavior, particularly nonstandard usages, or in attempts to widen types of approved behavior. Doubtless too, the experience of freshman composition in college reinforces the same linguistic myths as students are encouraged to strive to employ the exact noun or adjective, to use varied sentences, and so on, all done within a very traditional framework.

Regardless of what happens or does not happen in the public schools, many prospective teachers are required to take a course in English grammar either to qualify for certification or to satisfy academic advisors. The motives for such a requirement vary. In a few cases the pressure to take such a course results from the fact that linguistics is currently in vogue in several important groups of professional educators and it is considered in much the same way as audio-visual education or programmed instruction. In many cases though, perhaps even the majority, there is a genuine desire to have modern linguistic ideas introduced into the schools so that children might gain practical benefits from the insights derived from linguistic study. The reasoning is that although the study of traditional grammar did not bring about significant improvement in students' use of language in oral and written work, the study of structural or generative-transformational grammar might bring about such improvement. The commitment in this case is a long-term one. In still other cases the motivation is part of a general concern to help bring about radical change in the education of students by allowing them the experience of intellectual inquiry into a profoundly important area of their existence, a type of inquiry, moreover, which does not require expensive laboratories and apparatus, but which may still be made as demanding and perhaps ultimately as beneficial as any in the physical and social sciences.

THE PROBLEM OF COURSE CONTENT

The foregoing comments concern one set of problems associated with the study of grammar or linguistics. Such study has an uncertain place at all levels in our educational system. Like the famous Duke of York, it is neither up nor down. However, to be neither up nor down is to be in a most uncertain, possibly untenable, position vulnerable from all directions, vulnerable to changes in graduation and certification requirements, to priorities of departmental budgeting, and to the whims and fancies of various individuals. But if the place of grammar is uncertain, the problem of which grammar or grammars to teach if grammar is taught and of how to teach that grammar or grammars is just as difficult to solve.

There is not just one English grammar because there is not just one grammatical theory. There are grammatical theories and the consequence is that there are English grammars. Any examination of the content of courses in English grammar will reveal that five students coming from different institutions (or from the same institution if it is sufficiently large) showing course credit in "Modern English Grammar" may not necessarily have done the same kind of work, read the same texts, or even been asked to consider the same problems. It is even possible that they will not share a single experience in common. One may have studied Jespersen's *Essentials of English Grammar* (1933) along with Fries' *The Structure of English* (1952), the second Trager and Smith's *An Outline of English Structure* (1957) along with Hill's *Introduction to Linguistic Structures* (1958), the third Francis' *The Structure of American English* (1958) and the early Chomsky of *Syntactic Structures*

(1957), the fourth the recent Chomsky of *Aspects of the Theory of Syntax* (1965) along with Thomas' *Transformational Grammar and the Teacher of English* (1967), and the last Langendoen's *Essentials of English Grammar* (1970) and Jacobs and Rosenbaum's *English Transformational Grammar* (1968). Moreover, it is impossible to say which student has taken the best course by the criteria of textbook selection and course content alone.

The last remark is not one that is made lightly, for it implies that the various grammars mentioned all have some value and that the main variable may be that of presentation. The remark, therefore, needs to be examined to see whether or not it is justified. Can one really defend teaching grammatical theories associated with Fries, Trager and Smith, and Francis in 1968? Is it not true that a grammar based on distributional criteria alone is inadequate, that the Trager and Smith phonology is just too "hocus-pocus" to be acceptable, and that immediate-constituent analysis really has little to say about how sentences are produced and understood in all their infinite variety? Would it not be much wiser to teach only more recently developed theories? But if so, what theory should be taught, for among those theories must be numbered generative-transformational, generative-semantic, stratificational, neo-Firthian, and tagmemic theories, to name some of the principal contenders in the English-speaking world? Each theory has its ardent proponents and its fierce critics. That such strong feelings can be aroused by linguistic theory might, and does, puzzle many people who reason that if linguistics is a science, one might suppose that linguists be scientifically dispassionate in their inquiries. However, we should be aware that scientists are not entirely dispassionate, a fact brought out in some recent accounts of scientific theorizing, particularly those by Kuhn in *The Structure of Scientific Revolutions* (1962) and Watson in *The Double Helix* (1968). Scientists often hold passionately to their beliefs and scientific changes apparently are as often revolutionary as evolutionary. Consequently, in order to evaluate the quality of a course in Modern English grammar, it seems better to consider what view of the nature of linguistic (and presumably of scientific) inquiry was conveyed to the student than what particular subject matter or theoretical approach was used. Was Fries taught as the last word in English syntax? Was the Trager and Smith vowel system revealed as an instance of pure and shining truth? Was immediate-constituent analysis shown to be the key to all syntactic understanding? Was deep structure shown to be either entirely necessary or entirely unnecessary? And so on. Or were the grammars taught as particular instances of the scientific quest, so that the grammar taught was examined for the assumptions that were made, the procedures that were followed, the rigor that was demonstrated, and the questions that were raised?

There can be little doubt that a student who wished to continue in linguistics would be far better equipped to continue following a course using an immediate-constituent-type grammar taught by someone who approached the problem of teaching about linguistics as a process of inquiry into language than following a course using a generative grammar taught by someone who regarded generative grammar as a version of latter-day revelation. It should be noted that the two grammars singled out here, immediate-constituent and generative, are not singled out because they must necessarily be taught in the way just mentioned. It is just as easy to teach Francis with finality and Chomsky with charity as it is to do the opposite. Currently, generative grammarians have no monopoly on the truth, for some of the opponents of generative grammar are every bit as dogmatic defenders of a faith as are some of its proponents. However, a choice between a dogmatic generative presentation and a flexible neo-Bloomfieldian one is in effect no choice, for science and dogma cannot coexist.

If we agree that we must avoid a dogmatic approach to teaching, what should the content of a course be like and how should it be oriented? In a course which lasts only a single quarter or semester it is obviously quite impossible to teach more than a small part of what is known about English grammar; therefore, some selection is mandatory. If the course has no linguistics prerequisite, and such is generally the case, further complications ensue, for the course then has also to be an introductory course in linguistics, or at least in those linguistic ideas relevant to the grammar or grammars chosen for presentation. Various possible solutions exist. The instructor can present a once-over-lightly historical survey of ideas on English grammar from perhaps the eighteenth century to current work, injecting a few linguistic terms as he goes along. Such an approach has its merits since the continuity of linguistic ideas can be shown and the development of current controversies revealed; however, the result is more likely to be both poor linguistic history and poor linguistics. To guarantee at least an acceptable minimum of success such as approach almost certainly requires a two-semester sequence to produce some real sophistication about grammar rather than the memorization of terms and trends.

An alternative procedure is for the instructor to take two different grammatical theories, possible a Trager-and-Smith-type grammar and a Chomsky-type grammar, in order to constrast these. Again, a thorough and honest contrast of two very different grammars requires that students have considerable linguistic sophistication to begin with. The danger always exists that in the absence of such sophistication one model may be used as the foil, even the straw man, for the other so that a fair constrast of goals and procedures is not achieved. If it is possible to make a fair comparison of two such different grammars in one semester and, in doing so, provide students with the linguistic tools and insights to do similar work themselves, then there would be little to criticize in such an approach. However, it is extremely doubtful that such an objective can be achieved in a single semester in those circumstances which do not demand of the students one or more prerequisite linguistics courses.

THE OPENNESS OF THEORY

Circumstances almost always compel the instructor to resort to teaching one grammar whilst disregarding others so that he may achieve some thoroughness. Such an approach is after all linguistically and pedagogically honest in that students may thereby acquire some degree of expertise. The crucial problem for the instructor is that he is fully aware of the limited time that is available to him. If he believes he knows what linguistic inquiry is all about, what the best available grammatical theory is, and what an English grammar should look like, he is only human when he chooses to let such beliefs guide him in structuring his course. But, as already indicated, the instructor does incur an obligation not to propagandize against other theories because if education is not just the conveying of information, no more is it propagandizing for a particular narrow point of view. Education is concerned with free inquiry, and it should not matter which theory the instructor chooses if he keeps this point in mind. Many linguists would favor an English grammar based on a generative theory and there are very good reasons for making such a choice, but no matter which choice a particular instructor makes he must try to present the grammar for what it is, a theory not the truth, and present it with humility not arrogance.

There is always the danger too that the clientele of the course will influence the content of the course in undesirable ways. If, for example, the course is taken mainly by education majors, there might be pressures from education faculty and the students themselves to make the course "practical." Some of us have had the experience of teaching in such a situation and being subjected to such pressures. The pressures must be resisted and resisted strongly. "How can I apply what I am learning in the classroom?" is a question which should be asked only after a considerable amount of learning has taken place. Too often the practical-minded person wants answers to practical questions at the first or second class meeting long before he is in a position to recognize either the profundity of his questions or their irrelevance. No benefit is gained by giving such a student superficial answers of half truths. The situation is not unlike the one in which a linguist sometimes finds himself when, asked to address a group of teachers on the implications of linguistic research for the teaching of elementary school English, he finds he must do it in thirty minutes rather than thirty hours. The result is a crisis of conscience. Does he state a few generalizations, give a few gimmicks, and leave the impression that that is all linguistics is, or does he show how important it is to find the right questions to ask and how difficult it is to find good answers?

A course in Modern English grammar should be a course of this latter kind. It should open minds not close them. It should show the excitement of a new and growing discipline and not merely tinker with the dogmas of an old faith. And it should be unashamedly oriented toward theory, for theory is important. Knowing what one might ask of a good linguistic theory would lead to an enormous step forward in our teaching of English. It is far more important that teachers know something about linguistic theory than that they know how many basic sentence patterns there are or how to teach children to change active sentences into passive sentences using a transformational formula, and so on.

In the long run, a good training in the theoretical issues involved in describing English and accounting for grammatical ability is likely to prove far better for classroom teachers than a course which indoctrinates them into one grammar or another. If we can be sure of one thing in linguistics, it is that views of grammar will change. Teachers should not reject linguistics because it is changing so rapidly. They should become interested in the reasons for change and in working out for themselves the practical consequences of a linguistics which is changing, just as they must come to terms with the fact that linguists can disagree among themselves. Linguistics, in that it is changing and that different points of view exist, is no different from any other branch of scientific endeavor. The problem seems to be less one of the discipline itself than one of the "world view" of the teacher and of the society in which he lives in their accommodation, or lack of accommodation, to the process of change.

CONCLUSION

A place must be found for a much wider teaching of grammar in colleges and universities and, ideally, English grammar should be taught in the English departments of those institutions. The study of grammar for its own sake is a humane study of the best kind and students should be encouraged to undertake the experience of inquiry into how their language works. However, grammatical study for its own sake has very doubtful prospects in the public schools, at least in the foreseeable future. The schools are not ready for it, nor are the linguistic resources to implement such study currently available. Then, too, the second problem of which grammar or grammars to teach remains. Selection is necessary because there are conflicting views about the nature and content of grammatical study. However, it would be foolish indeed to cry "a plague on all your houses," as some have done, because of such disagreements. Finally, if the study of grammar is justified because it is a humane study, then the same reasoning demands that the particular grammar or grammars chosen for study be studied in the humane spirit, a spirit of inquiry and openness, not one of superficiality and dogma. Perhaps this last challenge is the greatest of all.

part two

Linguistics and Spelling

chapter three
Sounds and Spellings:
Spellings and Sounds

The relationship between English spellings and English sounds has intrigued a vast number of people. It has led some to the conclusion that English is an "unphonetic" language, by which they mean that English letters do not consistently represent the same sounds, and it even led George Bernard Shaw to the observation that *ghoti* would be a possible spelling for *fish*. Others have tried more seriously to see the connection between spellings and sounds and, in doing so, have inquired into the history of English spelling conventions and the sound system of English.

The English spelling system is both alphabetic and morphemic: it is a morphophonemic system in which letters are used to represent sounds in ways which preserve important morphemic units. Thus, even though sets like *Canada-Canadian*, *electric-electricity-electrical-electrician*, and *photograph-photographic-photographer* contain members with quite different sounds and stresses, English spelling conventions maintain the shapes of the fundamental meaning parts in each set: *Canada*, *electric*, and *photograph*. Since English spelling has a morphophonemic base, some of the attempts to describe the system in terms of phoneme-grapheme correspondences alone have not been very insightful, particularly when they have been based on rather shaky phonemic analyses.

SOUND TO SPELLING

Figure 1 gives the phonemes in one major dialect of English in the Trager-Smith notation together with the dictionary "pronunciation" equivalent for each phoneme and most of its spelling representations. In effect Figure 1 comes close to exhausting what can be said about sound to spelling relationships using the Trager-Smith phonemic system unless one wants to discuss certain spelling patterns that occur: the use of double letters, as in *bigger* and *stopping*; the relationship of vowel letter, consonant letter, *e* spellings (VC*e*) to a particular set of vowels, as in *cape*, *Pete*, and *tune*; the reasons for the various spellings of the schwa vowel; and so on.

It would be possible to use this information in a variety of ways in order to teach spelling. Each sound could be identified and its most frequent representations taught. For example, / æ / (a) is usually written with an *a*, as in *tap*, whereas /ey/ (ā) is usually written *aCe*, as in *tape*, although it can be represented by *ai*, *ay*, or *aigh*, as in *pail*, *day*, and *straight*. Letter-doubling conventions could be taught: *rap* and *rapping*, *rob* and *robbed*, and *big* and *bigger*. Stress could be discussed to make students alert to the many possible representations of schwa, as in the second syllables of *coma*, *taken*, *pencil*, *lemon*, and *helpful*. Historical reasons could be given for spellings such as *knee,psychology*, and *laugh*. And a fair number of other observations could be made too. However, it is doubtful that either a spelling program or a reading program should depend on a unidirectional approach from sound to spelling. A lot would be gained by also considering spelling to sound relationships.

Phoneme(s)	Dictionary Notation	Examples
Vowels		
æ	a	*at*, b*a*d
ey	ā	*ape*, *a*corn, p*ai*n, d*ay*, th*ey*, w*eigh*
ah	ä	f*a*ther, c*a*r
e	e	*e*nd, p*e*t, br*ea*d
iy	ē	P*e*te, m*e*, f*ee*t, m*ea*t, p*ie*ce, rec*ei*ve, final*ly*
i	i	*i*t, p*i*g
ay	ī	*i*ce, f*i*nal, l*i*e, m*y*
a	o	*o*dd, h*o*t
ow	ō	n*o*te, *o*ld, *oa*t, l*ow*, t*oe*
ɔ	ô	*o*ffice, f*o*rk, *au*thor, l*aw*, *a*ll
u	oo	w*oo*d, p*u*t

uw	$\overline{oo}$	f*oo*l, r*u*de, tr*ue*
oy	oi	*oi*l, b*oy*
aw	ou	*ou*t, c*ow*
ə (stressed)	u	*u*p, m*u*d, *o*ven, l*o*ve
yuw	$\bar{u}$	*u*se, c*ue*, f*ew*, f*eu*d
ər (stressed)	ur	t*ur*n, t*er*m, b*ir*d, w*or*d
ə (unstressed)	ə	*a*go, tak*e*n penc*i*l, lem*o*n, helpf*u*l
ər (unstressed)	ər	work*er*, li*ar*, pict*ure*, sail*or*

Consonants

b	b	*b*at, a*b*ove, jo*b*, ru*bb*er
č	ch	*ch*in, su*ch*, ha*tch*, na*tu*re
d	d	*d*ear, so*d*a, ba*d*, la*dd*er, play*ed*
f	f	*f*ive, de*f*end, lea*f*, o*ff*, *ph*iloso*ph*y, laug*h*
g	g	*g*ame, a*g*o, fo*g*, bi*gg*er, *gh*ost, *gu*est
h	h	*h*it, a*h*ead
ǰ	j	*j*oke, en*j*oy, e*dg*e, *g*em
k	k	*k*it, ba*k*ing, see*k*, tac*k*, *c*at, pi*c*nic, s*ch*ool
l	l	*l*id, sai*l*or, fee*l*, ba*ll*, a*ll*ow
m	m	*m*an, fa*m*ily, drea*m*, ha*mm*er, la*m*b, hy*mn*
n	n	*n*ot, fi*n*al, o*n*, ba*nn*er, *gn*at, *kn*ee, *pn*eumonia
ŋ	ng	si*ng*er, lo*ng*, si*n*k

p	p	*p*ail, re*p*air, soa*p*, su*pp*er
r	r	*r*ide, pa*r*ent, fou*r*, a*rr*ow, *wr*ite
s	s	*s*at, a*s*ide, cat*s*, *c*ent, pa*ss*, *sc*ience, *p*sychology
š	sh	*sh*oe, wi*sh*ing, fi*sh*, *s*ure, na*ti*on
t	t	*t*ag, pre*t*end, ha*t*, bu*tt*er, pass*ed*
θ	th	*th*in, e*th*er, bo*th*
ð̌	*th*	*th*is, mo*th*er, smoo*th*
v	v	*v*ery, fa*v*or, ha*ve*
w	w	*w*et, re*w*ard, (sometimes *wh*ich)
y	y	*y*es
z	z	*z*oo, ga*z*ing, ja*zz*, ro*s*e, dog*s*
ž	zh	trea*s*ure, sei*z*ure, gara*ge*

Figure 1: Spelling Representations of English Phonemes

SPELLING TO SOUND

The first point to be observed is that English consonants do not really create much of a problem in proceeding from spelling to sound in any attempt to decide how a particular text is to be pronounced. The problem is really one of determining what sounds individual vowel letters, vowel letter combinations, and vowel letters in combination with letters such as *y*, *w*, and *gh* represent in words. The discussion that follows employs the terms *short* and *long* in the senses used in the literature on phonics and reading instructions.

Figure 2 shows typical *short* pronunciations of single vowel letters in certain distributional patterns. From Figure 2 we can see that a single vowel letter represents a *short* pronunciation before two or more consonants (-CC), or before a single consonant at the end of a word (-C #).

Figure 3 shows typical *long* pronunciations of single vowel letters in certain distributional patterns. A single vowel letter represents a *long* pronunciation before a single consonant plus a vowel (-CV), or before a single consonant, plus *r* or *l* plus a vowel (-C $\frac{r}{l}$ V).

Letter	Phoneme	Dictionary Notation	−CC	−C#
a	æ	a	pl*a*nt, b*a*ttle	b*a*t
e	e	e	b*e*nt, s*e*ttle	b*e*t
i	i	i	m*i*st, l*i*ttle	b*i*t
y	i	i	m*y*th	g*y*m
o	a	o	p*o*nd, b*o*ttle	h*o*t
u	ə	u	b*u*nch, s*u*pple	b*u*t

Note that *a* before *l* plus a consonant represents / ɔ / (ô): *bald, ball*
Note that *i* before *ld* and *nd* also often represents /ay/ (ī): *wild*
Note that *o* before *l* plus a consonant represents /ow/ (ō): *bold*
Note that *u* between *p*, *b*, and *f* and *l*, *sh*, and *tch* represents /u/ (oo): *bull, push, Butch*

Figure 2: Short Pronunciations of Single English Vowel Letters

Letter	Phonemes	Dictionary Notation	−CV	−C $\frac{r}{l}$ V
a	ey	ā	h*a*te	t*a*ble, *a*cre
e	iy	ē	P*e*te	*ze*bra
i	ay	ī	k*i*te	b*i*ble, m*i*tre
y	ay	ī	t*y*pe	c*y*cle
o	ow	ō	v*o*te	n*o*ble
u	yuw, uw	ū, o͞o	m*u*le, t*u*ne	p*u*trid

Figure 3: Long Pronunciations of Single English Vowel Letters

Figure 4 shows the typical pronunciations of vowel letters in word-final position. At the end of a word (-#) or before an *e* at the end of a word (-*e*#), a vowel letter represents the pronunciations given in Figure 4. Figure 5 shows the distribution of the pronunciations of single vowel letters before *r* plus a vowel (-*r*V). Figure 6 shows the distribution of the pronunciations of single vowel letters before *r* at the end of a word (-*r*#) or before *r* plus a consonant (-*r*C).

Figure 7 shows the pronunciations of various vowel-vowel and vowel-consonant combinations. The data in Figure 7 adequately testify to the fact that the reading teacher's adage that "when two vowels go walking the first one does the talking" is reasonably correct even if rather naively expressed. In general, vowel digraphs do represent *long* pronunciations of the first vowel: *pail, meet, feet, tied, boat,* and *suit.* The major exceptions are *oi, oy, oo, ou,* and *ow,* as in *boil, boy, foal, loud,* and *now.*

Letter	Phoneme(s)	Dictionary Notation	−#	−*e*#
a	ah	ä	sp*a*	
e	iy	ē	m*e*	fl*ee*
i	ay	ī	H*i*	t*ie*
y	ay	ī	m*y*	B*y*e B*y*e
o	ow	ō	n*o*	t*o*e
u	yuw, uw	ū, o͞o	St*u*	d*u*e

Figure 4: Pronunciations of Vowel Letters in Word-Final Position

Letters	Phonemes	Dictionary Notation	−*r*V
ar	er	är	h*a*re
er	ir	ēr	h*e*re
ir	ayr	ir̄	h*i*re
yr	ayr	ir̄	l*y*re
or	or	ōr, ôr	p*o*re
ur	yur, ur	ūr, o͞or	p*u*re, s*u*re

Figure 5: Pronunciations of Single Vowel Letters before rV

Letters	Phonemes	Dictionary Notation	—r#	—rC
ar	ar	är	f*ar*	c*a*rt
er	ər	ur	h*er*	f*e*rn
ir	ər	ur	s*ir*	sh*i*rt
yr	ər	ur		m*y*rhh
or	or	ôr	f*or*	f*o*rt
ur	ər	ur	f*ur*	h*u*rt

Note that *ar* after *w* represents /or/ (ôr): *war*
Note that *or* after *w* represents /ər/ (ur): *word*
Figure 6: Pronunciations of Single Vowel Letters before r # or rC

Vowel Digraphs	Phoneme(s)	Dictionary Notation	Examples
ai, ay, aigh	ey	ā	p*ai*l, d*ay*, str*aigh*t
au, aw, augh	ɔ	ô	t*au*t, l*aw*, t*augh*t
ea	iy	ē	b*ea*t
ee	iy	ē	b*ee*t
ei, ey, eigh	ey	ā	v*ei*n, th*ey*, w*eigh*
eu, ew	yuw, uw	ū, ōō	f*eu*d, n*ew*
ie	iy	ē	bel*ie*ve
oa	ow	ō	b*oa*t
oi, oy	oy	oi	b*oi*l, b*oy*
oo	uw, u	ōō, oo	f*oo*l, w*oo*d
ou, ow, ough	aw, ow	au, ō	l*ou*d, n*ow*, kn*ow*, th*ough*
ui	yuw, uw, i	ū, ōō, i	s*ui*t, b*ui*ld
ui	ay	ī	b*uy*

Figure 7: Pronunciations of Various Vowel-Vowel and Vowel-Consonant Combinations

SOME BASIC RELATIONSHIPS

It is also possible to use some of the above data in ways which show how systematically English spellings represent English sounds. Not only do certain spelling patterns occur time and time again, but also sets of relationships exist between many words and their derivatives.

One important pattern is that which contrasts vowel, consonant, *e* (VC*e*), in which the vowel is a *long* vowel, with vowel, consonant, space (VC #) or vowel, consonant, consonant (VCC), in which the vowel is a *short* vowel. Some typical examples are as follows:

hate	hat
lane	land
bake	back
Pete	pet
scene	send
eke	deck
wine	win
line	lint
bile	bill
rote	rot
bone	bond
cone	cock
cute	cut
rune	runt
mule	mull

A variant of this pattern has vowels other than *e* occurring after the single consonant, so that in addition to examples such as *hate, Pete, wine, rote,* and *cute,* from the above list there are also examples such as *halo, veto, silo, coma,* and *Hugo.*

The consonant-doubling convention before certain suffixes allows for the vowels in the following pairs of words to be distinguished: *raped, rapped; wining, winning; lobed, lobbed;* and *cuter, cutter.* Single vowels before *r* (*-r*) and single vowels before *l* and a consonant (*-lC*) fall into patterns. Before *r* most single vowels are pronounced with a schwa: *her, fir, worm,* and *turn.* The exceptions are *a* (*far, war*) and *o* (*for*). Before *l* and a consonant most single vowels are pronounced with their *short* values: *belt, bell, silt, bill, fudge,* and *gull.* The exceptions are *a* (*walk, ball*) and *o* (*colt, poll*).

It is possible to devise other patterns too, many of which can be abstracted from the information given earlier. These patterns testify to the systematic nature of English spelling. However, it is also possible to show how English words and their derivatives maintain their morphemic resemblance in that the spellings remain unchanged even though the pronunciations change. Because English vowel letters can represent more than one sound, a word and its derivatives may have different vowel sounds (among other changes) yet still retain the same vowel letter for the different sounds. Very systematic patterning can be observed in English, as follows:

a	/ey/ (ā)	/æ/ (a)
	sane	sanity
	urbane	urbanity
	humane	humanity
	angel	angelic
	fable	fabulous
	state	static
	radius	radical

e	/iy/ (ē)	/e/ (e)
	serene	serenity
	meter	metric
	discreet	discretion
	intervene	intervention
	convene	convention
	penal	penalty
	obscene	obscenity

i, y	/ay/ (ī)	/i/ (i)
	rise	risen
	reside	residual
	decide	decision
	sign	signal
	wild	wilderness
	type	typical
	cycle	cyclic

o   /ow/   (ō)   /a/   (o)

tone	tonic
verbose	verbosity
holy	holiday
mediocre	mediocrity
neurosis	neurotic
mode	modesty
dispose	disposition

u   /yuw, uw/ (ū, ōō)   /ə/   (u)

reduce	reduction
conducive	conduction
induce	induction
deduce	deduction
presume	presumption
consume	consumption
assume	assumption

We can also add words with *ea* spelling to the pattern with *e* spellings:

                                 /iy/   (ē)   /e/   (e)

clean	cleanse
breathe	breath
deal	dealt
steal	stealth
please	pleasure
mean	meant
heal	health

CONCLUSION

Chomsky and Halle (1968), Venezky (1967), and others have very adequately documented some of the systematic relationships that exist between spellings and sounds. Any spelling program, phonics program, or program for teaching English pronunciation to speakers of other languages should be based, in part at least, on a recognition of that relationship. It is not enough to exploit sound to spelling relationships; it is not enough to approach English spelling as though it were largely chaotic; it is not enough to assume that pronunciation facts can best be learned by ignoring spelling facts. Truly adequate programs will recognize both sound-to-spelling and spelling-to-sound relationships, the systematic nature of both the sound system and the spelling system, the fit between the two, and the morphophonemic basis of English orthography.

part three

Linguistics and Reading

chapter four
Linguistic Insights into Reading

Within applied linguistics the topic of linguistics and reading is of great interest for several reasons. First of all, it forces us to discuss some of the difficulties involved in attempts to use insights from research in theoretical linguistics in the solution of a practical problem, in this case that of teaching children to read and of understanding the reading process. In other cases the problem may be one of teaching a foreign language, of translating a text, or of choosing a national language. Just what linguistic knowledge is relevant and how may relevant knowledge best be used? Those linguists who have been interested in the problem have adopted a variety of different approaches because they have viewed it differently and suscribed to different ideas about the proper nature of linguistic inquiry.

The second reason which makes this topic interesting is that it allows us to observe some of the limitations of the uses of linguistic knowledge. Some indication will be given of specific areas in which the limits of linguistic knowledge are reached and in which other kinds of knowledge are required. It is apparent that certain linguists have confused non-linguistic matters with linguistic ones, possibly to the extent of over-reaching themselves. Such over-reaching is not unique to linguists: experts from other disciplines also speak on topics outside their field of competence with the same air of authority they assume within that field.

The third reason is no less important than the first two: it is to show how linguistics itself is changing in its concerns, its techniques, and its rhetoric. This last statement will become clearer when the approaches to the reading process taken by Bloomfield and Fries are compared with those taken by Chomsky and Halle. The content and the style of their discussions of the problem differ widely; however, there is some reason to say that the conclusions of Bloomfield and Fries on the one hand and those of Chomsky and Halle on the other may not actually be so very far apart.

LEONARD BLOOMFIELD

The earliest proposals to use modern linguistic knowledge in the teaching of reading apparently came from Leonard Bloomfield, who was disturbed by certain aspects of school instruction, particularly the instruction given in language and in reading. For example, in a statement published in the very first volume of *Language* in 1925 explaining in part why the Linguistic Society of America had been founded, he wrote as follows:

> Our schools are conducted by persons who, from professors of education down to teachers in the classroom, know nothing of the results of linguistic science, not even the relation of writing to speech or of standard language to dialect. In short, they do not know what language is, and yet must teach it, and in consequence waste years of every child's life and reach a poor result (Bloomfield, 1925, p.5).

Bloomfield felt that the methods being used to teach his son to read were unenlightened and revealed a lack of knowledge about language. Consequently, he devised his own method of teaching his son to read and shared his opinions, method, and materials with those of his friends who had like interests. These later became known as the Bloomfield system for teaching reading when they found their way into *Let's Read* (Bloomfield and Barnhart, 1961).

Bloomfield rejected the "code-breaking" approach known as phonics as a way of teaching reading, claiming that the proponents of phonics confused statements about speech with those about writing to the point that they often appeared to be teaching children to speak, whereas all they were really doing was teaching them to associate written symbols with already known words. He objected to practices such as breaking up words into smaller parts corresponding to letters, crediting individual letters with having sounds, sounding out words (for example, *cat* as [kə æ tə]), and blending sounds in an attempt to decode written words. Not only did Bloomfield reject a "code-breaking," or phonics, approach but he also rejected the competing "whole-word," or global, approach, claiming that it ignored the alphabetic nature of the English writing system in that it treated English as though it were Chinese.

Bloomfield believed that children learning to read should first be trained in visual discrimination and then be taught to associate visually discriminated objects, letters, and word shapes to already known sounds and meanings. The story line (that is the meaning of the reading materials) was, he believed, far less important than the regularity of the connection between sounds and symbols (that is the phoneme-grapheme correspondences). Therefore, in order to guarantee that children should easily acquire a mastery of these correspondences, Bloomfield insisted that they be trained to discriminate in a left-to-right direction and to name the letters of the alphabet without error. He believed that requiring children to name the letters in new words from left to right guaranteed both visual discrimination and correct word attack. Just as linguists, and presumably children (intuitively in their case), could segment an utterance into phonemes, beginning readers had to learn to segment words into graphemes, and the teacher systematically had to teach children to relate the two discrimination abilities. The Bloomfield approach is, therefore, one which is based on the introduction of regular sound-symbol, or phoneme-grapheme, correspondences so that children can acquire the fundamental understanding they must acquire in order to read, that writing is a representation of speech, and, on the whole, quite a systematic one.

Bloomfield was also concerned with the notion of contrast, seeing a need to teach whole written words such as *can, van,* and *fan* in contrast with each other and to introduce all the contrastive details of the English writing system gradually and systematically so that the child learning to read would realize, as Bloomfield wrote, that *"printed letter = speech sound to be spoken"* (Bloomfield and Barnhart, 1961, p.36). It is not surprising therefore that the resulting lists, exercises, and testing materials look something like the "word family" lists found in many of the old-fashioned nineteenth century readers. For example, some testing materials from *Let's Read* are constructed as follows:

> ban, can, Dan, fan, gan,...
> bat, cat, fat, gat, hat,...
> bad, cad, dad, fad, gad,...
> bap, cap, dap, gap, Hap,...
> bag, cag, dag, fag, gag,... (Bloomfield and Barnhart, 1961, p. 101).

According to Bloomfield, the basic task confronting the child who is learning to read is mastery of the spelling system of English not of the meanings of English words and sentences. Therefore, teachers may use nonsense syllables and nonsense words in order to allow their students to achieve such mastery:

> Tell the child that the nonsense syllables are parts of real words which he will find in the books that he reads. For example, the child will know *han* in *handle* and *jan* in *January* and *mag* in *magnet* or *magpie*. The acquisition of

nonsense syllables is an important part of the task of mastering the reading process (Bloomfield and Barnhart, 1961, pp.41-42).

Another linguist, Robert Hall (1964), gives much the same kind of advice claiming that the "ultimate test of any method of teaching reading is whether the learners can deal with nonsense syllables . . . " (p.432). Both Bloomfield and Hall are really advocating an emphasis on a "code-breaking" approach, but not the particular "code-breaking" approach known as phonics. In his work, Bloomfield was concerned almost exclusively with monosyllabic words, and polysyllabic words received very little attention. In defense of this emphasis he claimed that his son found no difficulty in transferring to polysyllabic words once he had achieved a mastery of the monosyllabic patterns.

Believing that the major task the beginning reader must master is one wholly concerned with the interpretation of words and not one concerned with guessing at the meanings of words by using accompanying illustrations, Bloomfield rejected the use of illustrations in reading materials on the grounds that they are either irrelevant or misleading. Some of the materials for teaching reading that Fries and his followers were to develop following Bloomfield's example likewise do not contain pictures so that children could be left free to focus their attention on the words themselves rather than on the accompanying illustrations. The results of applying Bloomfield's theories to reading are materials like the following:

A rap. A gap.
Dad had a map.
Pat had a bat.
Tad had a tan cap.
Nan had a tan hat.
Nan had a fat cat.
A fat cat ran at a bad rat (Bloomfield and Barnhart, 1963, p.37).

Bloomfield's ideas on reading contain much that is admirable. First of all, his work on English phoneme-grapheme correspondences was based on a good knowledge of the important surface phonological contrasts in English. Bloomfield also stressed the fact that the English writing system is basically an alphabetic one and that it is not as inconsistent as it is often made out to be, particularly when approached from the viewpoint of *how sounds are represented in writing* and not from that of how letters are pronounced, or, even worse, how letters *should* be pronounced. Then, too, his work contains a welcome insistence that some of the basic insights necessary to understand the reading process are to be found in linguistics. However, the Bloomfield system has much more to say about the linguistic *content* of reading materials than about an actual *method* of teaching reading. Bloomfield's comments on methodology seem to be based on an extrapolation of some procedures, such as contrast, which linguists have found useful in their work as linguists and not on procedures derived from teaching reading. This type of extrapolation is characteristic of much work in applied linguistics in general. It is certainly not unique to the problem of using linguistic insights in understanding the reading process or in the teaching of reading. Bloomfield was also rigidly behavioristic in the psychological theory he espoused.

CHARLES FRIES

A more recent proposal than Bloomfield's to use linguistic insights in reading was made by Charles Fries in *Linguistics and Reading* (1963), probably the most influential book on linguistics and reading published to date. Like Bloomfield, Fries took the position that reading experts are quite unfamiliar with linguistics and in general exhibit little knowledge of language at all; consequently, he set out to correct this defect and to offer an outline of a method for teaching reading that drew heavily on linguistic insights in a manner reminiscent of the approach behind his well-known book on second-language teaching *Teaching and Learning English as a Foreign Language* (1945).

One important distinction that Fries insisted on is in the use of the terms *phonics, phomemics,* and *phonetics,* and he devoted a whole chapter to the problem of clarifying the differences among these terms and setting the record straight. He cites numerous examples of the confused use of the three terms in the literature on reading in a telling indictment of most writing on the subject of phonics, that is of most writing on the "code-breaking" view of reading. Like Bloomfield before him, Fries emphasized that written English is alphabetic in nature and that English spelling is not inconsistent if statements about speech and statements about writing are clearly distinguished and if letters (graphemes) are regarded as representations of significant speech sounds (phonemes). Fries pointed out some of the regular spelling patterns in English and said that it was the reading teacher's task to teach these to beginning readers by presenting them in carefully arranged sequences and by giving beginning readers considerable practice in recognizing them in contrasting words.

Fries considered that in learning to read, children had to master a new visual task, in which they had to associate visual responses quite automatically with previously discriminated auditory responses. He believed that this process, which he regarded as a transfer process, required visual training, for example training in left-to-right eye movements and in the discrimination of the distinguishing features of letters and words. For this reason Fries rejected the concurrent introduction of both upper and lower case letters in beginning texts in favor of the exclusive use of upper case letters so as to reduce the burden of discrimination for the child who was learning to read. He apparently rejected the argument that the elimination of ascenders and descenders and the resultant uniform "block" shapes of written words might result in the loss of many useful visual clues and would reduce the amount of visual information available to the child. Instead, Fries believed that children would find written words composed out of twenty-six uniform letters easier to perceive than the corresponding words composed out of twice that number of letters. Later he modified this view.

Fries also insisted on the use of contrastive word patterns since he believed that the principle of contrast was basic to both linguistic structure and visual perception. He rejected the spelling out of words that Bloomfield recommended, insisting instead that the critically important skill for children to acquire is one of being able to make visual discriminations between whole words and between whole patterns or units of meaning. He sought, therefore, to minimize any factor which would tend to require children to focus on units smaller than whole words. Although Fries recognized that written English is alphabetic and the alphabet is a contrastive system, he claimed that the more important system of contrasts was the one associated with words and meanings; consequently, his method was essentially a "whole-word" method rather than a "phonics" method of the traditional kind. Fries also stressed the importance of oral reading in the belief that the written message is a representation of the oral message; however, his goal was still most definitely silent reading in the later stages of the program. The following is an example of a page from one of the Fries readers, as these were later developed from his ideas:

The Cat on the Van.

Dan is on the van.
Nat is on the van.
The pat is on the van.

The cat can bat the pan.
Dan can pat the cat.
The man ran the van (Fries, Fries, Wilson, and Rudolph, 1966, p.36).

Like Bloomfield, Fries had very little to say about comprehension; both apparently regarded comprehension as a basically passive activity highly dependent on oral language skills. Children must learn to react instantly to the contrasts between *mat* and *mate* and between *bit* and *beat*. They already react to the differences between these words when they are spoken. What they must do in learning to read is to associate a visual pattern which they have learned to discriminate from other visual patterns to a speech pattern which they already know and can discriminate from other speech patterns. A child who is learning to read is already subconsciously aware of the different kinds of meanings and patterns in his language or he could not communicate in that language. What he needs to have unlocked for him is the code that is writing, so that he can have access to these different kinds of meanings and patterns through the medium of print. Fries went so far as to claim that this code can be unlocked for the beginning reader within a year of his learning to "talk satisfactorily," an age which he put at four or five. Needless to say, this claim has appeared to be rather extravagant to many who actually teach reading. Fries, therefore, did not regard the problem of teaching reading comprehension as a serious one. He obviously took issue with wide-ranging definitions of the reading process which relate that process to social, psychological, and physiological factors in favor of a view of the reading process as a kind of high-speed visual recognition of meanings that are already familiar to the reader. Reading comprehension is, therefore, a specific instance of general linguistic comprehension.

Both Bloomfield and Fries strongly insisted that a particular kind of linguistic knowledge is of paramount importance in gaining insight into the reading process and in determining the content of a reading series. They also assumed that principles of linguistic analysis, such as patterning and contrast, can by extrapolation become useful principles in reading pedagogy. Henry Lee Smith (1963) has pointed out that there are certain valid pedagogical issues which linguists have tended to ignore when they have talked about reading: typography;

choice of illustrations; some repetition of patterns and words; and attention to both story line and characters. Smith cautions that it would be unwise for linguists who take an interest in reading to assume that reading teachers have learned nothing about teaching reading from their experiences, either individually or collectively. His words have been heeded to some extent in recent writings on linguistics and reading. They were obviously motivated in part by the hostility which characterized some of the original linguistics-reading discussions. That such hostility, particularly on the part of the reading experts, should have been aroused is not surprising when one reads some of the statements made by linguists about reading. For example, the statements by Bloomfield and Hall that there should be no illustrations in reading texts and the one by Fries that reading is a passive activity run counter to what most authorities on reading consider to be pedagogically sound observations. It must be emphasized that linguistics as a discipline has nothing to contribute to the discussion of whether or not there should be illustrations in a reading text: the inclusion or exclusion of illustrations is entirely a pedagogical decision. Likewise, any definition of the reading process as a passive process indicates a certain lack of awareness of the many problems inherent in the teaching of reading.

It would not be unfair to say that what has become known as the linguistic method of teaching reading in North America is one which relies heavily on the work of Bloomfield and Fries. In essence, the method entails little more than the presentation of regular phoneme-grapheme, or sound-spelling, relationships in beginning reading texts, in many ways a kind of neo-phonics. The materials developed by the followers of Bloomfield and Fries reflect this concern: these materials give no indication that the possible linguistic contribution to reading involves anything more than the systematic introduction of the regularities and irregularities of English spelling. There is, in fact, scarcely more than an occasional passing reference to any other than this one solitary point that linguists have made about English.

RICHARD VENEZKY

The concern for phoneme-grapheme correspondences and for the importance of these in teaching reading has led to many studies, some quite sophisticated, of the relationships of various phonological segments to various graphological segments. These studies vary in quality and purpose. One of the best has come from Richard

Venezky (1967), particularly because he has attempted to relate his work on correspondences to a model of the reading process. Venezky has done more than count phonemes and graphemes, compute frequencies of correspondence, and attempt to program a logical sequence of correspondences. Rather, he has attempted to construct a set of rules for translating orthographic symbols into speech sounds, because he considers it useful to characterize the reading process in those terms. His work is, therefore, an attempt to construct a partial model of the reading process which recognizes the distributions of phonemes and graphemes, the frequencies of occurrence, and the patterns of correspondences. Central to the model is a set of rules which relates all of these. Venezky writes of the process of learning to read as follows:

> Learning to read . . . requires primarily the translation from written symbols to sound, a procedure which is the basis of the reading process and is probably the only language skill unique to reading. . . . The patterns summarized here represent an ideal system for translating from spelling to sound . . . (p. 102).

He describes how the model works, as follows:

> As examples of how this model organizes spelling-to-sound rules, the processes for predicting the pronunciation of *social* and *signing* are shown below.

> *social* would be mapped into // sosɪæl // by the grapheme-to-morphophoneme rules for the separate units *s, o, c, i, a, l*. On the first morphophonemic level, the main word stress would be placed on the first syllable, resulting in // sósɪæl //. Then, through vowel reduction, // ɪæl // would become // jəl // and the resulting //sj// would be palatalized to // š //. The form // sóšəl // would then be mapped onto the phonemic level, giving / sóšəl /.

> *signing* would first be broken into *sign* and *ing* and then each of these graphemic allomorphs would be mapped onto the morphophonemic level, yielding //sɪgn// and //ɪng//. Upon combination of the two forms and the application of stress and certain phonotactical rules, the form //sɪgnɪŋg// would result. By rules for leveling consonant clusters, final //ŋg// would become //ŋ// and //gn// would become //n// with compensatory alternation of //ɪ// to //ɑɪ//. These operations yield //sɑɪnɪŋ// which is automatically mapped into /sɑɪnɪŋ/ (pp. 94-95).

Some very interesting differences exist between such an approach and that of Bloomfield and Fries. First of all, there is a concern with a level of representation called *morphophonemic*, a level which looks very like the standard orthography. Then, there is a set of ordered rules which, for example, assign stress and convert morphophonemes sometimes into morphophonemes but always eventually into phonemes. This last phonemic level is important in Venezky's work. He makes no attempt to eliminate it. Nor are the conversion rules necessarily made to conform to the demands of the kind of evaluation criterion that the generative-transformationalists insist on in their work. In the *signing* example, the morphophoneme $//\mathrm{I}//$ becomes the phonemes $/\mathrm{aI}/$ through an intermediate morphophonemic stage in an apparently idiosyncratic way that a computer can handle which is apparently unrelated to the way in which certain other morphophonemes attain their phonemic realizations. However, Venezky's work does recognize some important patterns of English orthography as, for example, in the following comment on the *a* grapheme and on the possible pedagogical consequences. Venezky points out that the letter *a* has two primary realizations in stressed position, $/\mathrm{æ}/$ and $/e/$, and he notes the orthographic and phonological relationships of pairs of words like *annal* and *anal*, *rat* and *rate*, and *sanity* and *sane*. He adds this comment:

> The Bloomfieldian sequencing begins with the $/\mathrm{æ}/$ pronunciation for *a*, introducing the $/e/$ pronunciation at a later time with no special emphasis on the relation between $/\mathrm{æ}/$ and $/e/$ when derived from *a*. An alternative to this approach is to present both pronunciations at once, working with such pairs as *rat:rate, mat:mate, fat:fate, hat:hate* and *man:mane*. Both the associations of *a* to $/\mathrm{æ}/$ and *a* to $/e/$ and the discrimination of the graphemic environments would be emphasized. Whether or not a child first learning to read can handle this task probably depends upon the pedagogy employed. The potential generalization derived from the differentiation approach, however, certainly is greater than that from the simple-sequence method (p. 103).

Venezky has added a further dimension to understanding the reading process beyond that of the contributions of Bloomfield and Fries. As is indicated in Figure 1, Bloomfield and Fries were concerned with a model of the process in which the beginning reader was required to establish a set of visual contrasts and then to associate this set of visual contrasts to a set of already known phonemic contrasts. Venezky is less concerned with such simple sets of contrasts and associations. As indicated in Figure 2, he favors drawing up a set of conversion rules rather than a set of association rules. Moreover, he is very much concerned with proceeding from writing to speech rather than from speech to writing.

In addition to postulating such a model of the process, Venezky also points out how pairs of lax and tense, or, in his terms, "checked" and "free," vowels relate to each other in English, in such word pairs as *fat:fate, met:mete, sit:site, rob:robe,* and *run:rune.* He stresses the fact that English orthographic conventions require the use of the same vowel letter in certain orthographic patterns, as with the *a* in *sane:sanity,* the *e* in *concede:concession,* and the *i* in *collide:collision,* but he makes no attempt to account for the patterning synchronically.

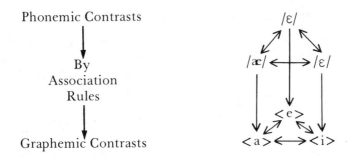

Figure 1: Bloomfield and Fries

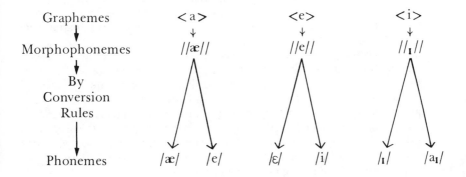

Figure 2: Venezky (continued on next page)

Example:

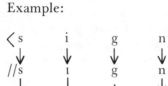

Figure 2: Venezky

NOAM CHOMSKY AND MORRIS HALLE

As is well known, the phonemic level of representation of so much interest to Bloomfield, Fries, and Venezky holds no attraction to Chomsky and Halle, who regard it as no more than the methodological artifact of a particular kind of linguistic inquiry which they have attacked repeatedly. Chomsky and Halle favor a level of representation which they call *systematic phonemic*, a level which they claim the standard orthography captures quite well. They write as follows on this point in *The Sound Pattern of English* (1968):

> There is, incidentally, nothing particularly surprising about the fact that conventional orthography is ... a near optimal system for the lexical representation of English words. The fundamental principle of orthography is that phonetic variation is not indicated where it is predictable by general rule. Thus, stress placement and regular vowel or consonant alternations are generally not reflected. Orthography is a system designed for readers who know the language, who understand sentences and therefore know the surface structure of sentences. Such readers can produce the correct phonetic forms, given the orthographic representation and the surface structure, by means of the rules that they employ in producing and interpreting speech. It would be quite pointless for the orthography to indicate these predictable variants. Except for unpredictable variants (e.g., *man-men, buy-bought*), an optimal orthography would have one representation for each lexical entry. Up to ambiguity, then, such a system would maintain a close correspondence between semantic units and orthographic representations (p. 49).

According to this claim, therefore, English orthography is a good orthography for a speaker who "knows" the language. Chomsky and Halle proceed to describe the reading process in the following terms, using the model indicated in Figure 3:

> [The] process of reading aloud . . . might . . . be described in the following way. We assume a reader who has internalized a grammar G of the language that he speaks natively. The reader is presented with a linear stretch W of written symbols, in a conventional orthography. He produces as an internal representation of this linear stretch W a string S of abstract symbols of the sort that we have been considering. Utilizing the syntactic and semantic information available to him, from a preliminary analysis of S, as well as much extra-linguistic information regarding the writer and the context, the reader understands the utterance, and, in particular, assigns to S a surface structure Σ. With Σ available, he can then produce the phonetic representation of S and, finally, the physical signal corresponding to the visual input W. Clearly, reading will be facilitated to the extent that the orthography used for W corresponds to the underlying representations provided by the grammar G. To the extent that these correspond, the reader can rely on the familiar phonological processes to relate the visual input W to an acoustic signal. Thus one would expect that conventional orthography should, by and large, be superior to phonemic transcription, which is in general quite remote from underlying lexical or phonological representation and not related to it by any linguistically significant set of rules... [Conventional orthography] can be read only when the surface structure (including the internal structure of words) is known, that is, when the utterance is to some degree understood (pp. 49-50).

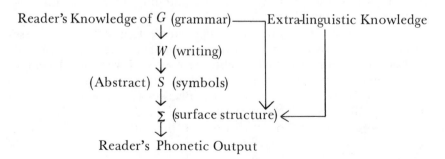

Figure 3: Chomsky and Halle

The Sound Pattern of English is primarily concerned with two problems. The first is a search for the best set of abstract phonological units to represent meaning units, that is a search for the best set of underlying lexical representations for English. The second is a search for the best set of rules to realize these systematic phonemes into phonetic output. The result of the first search is the postulation of a set of systematic phonemes which look remarkably like the set of phonemes postulated for Early Modern English. For example, the set of systematic vowel phonemes contains only monophthongal representations and uses both tense and lax and round and unround as distinctive features. The symbolization used by Chomsky and Halle looks very much the same as that of standard English orthography and neatly draws together both phonetically quite different vowels, such as those in *deduce* and *deduction, Canada* and *Canadian*, and *divine* and *divinity*, and variant pronunciations such as the well-known variant pronunciations of *ration, lever, sinecure,* and *progress.* The result of the search for the optimal set of phonological units or systematic phonemes is an extremely elegant and attractive system. The result of the second search for generative phonological rules is the postulation of a set of such rules which resemble, even in their clothing in distinctive features and a generative phonology, that set of rules other linguists have postulated to account for such phenomena as the Great Vowel Shift and other well-known sound changes.

The Sound Pattern of English is a rather convincing demonstration that it is possible to describe a vast amount of English phonology within the system the authors postulate. The demonstration of the need for two types of cluster, strong and weak, in determining stress placement, of the generality of the transformational rules, and of the importance of ordering and cycling in the application of the rules is undoubtedly an important contribution to linguistic theory. However, there are many *ad hoc* decisions and exceptions and certainly the main vocabulary discussed in *The Sound Pattern of English* is of Romance origin. Moreover, the authors make few claims either for the definiteness of the system, stating only that *The Sound Pattern of English* is a report on "work in progress" (p.vii), or for its psychological reality.

Some observations may be made about the proposals put forward by Chomsky and Halle. The first is that this type of theoretical work may really be of little or no use for gaining any insights at all into the reading process. Since Chomsky and Halle are largely concerned with vocabulary of Romance origin, what they have to say about such vocabulary adds little to any understanding of the processes involved in beginning reading. A beginning reader neither knows nor needs to know this vocabulary, and he certainly should not be taught it as part of the task of learning to read. His reading materials should be filled with vocabulary of Germanic origin, possibly of a simple monosyllabic variety. Certainly, it should not be words like *policy, politic, politicize, politico-economic, polyandrous, polyandry, polygamous, polygamy, polyhedral, polyhedrous, pond, Pontiac, pontificate,* and so on, which is one randomly selected sequence from the Word Index to *The Sound Pattern of English* (p.458). It is an interesting fact that most of us can pronounce these words correctly without even knowing what some of them mean, but they are, except for *pond,* not the words we would expect a six-year old to know or want him to read. Rather they are just the words we expect him to be able to read later when, as a result of learning to read, he is in the position of being able to read in order to learn. Much of Chomsky and Halle's description is valid only for a particular kind of person, a highly literate one. The crucial question is how much of such a rich system of phonology as that postulated in *The Sound Pattern of English* can we ascribe to a six-year old. Undoubtedly we must ascribe a great deal, for certainly a six-year old can assign stress correctly in a large number of cases, does reduce vowels automatically, and does make the majority of surface phonetic contrasts without difficulty. A six-year old undoubtedly possesses much of the basic phonological competence he will have as an adult. At the same time though, it is likely that the sets of rules that he uses and of lexical representations that he has at his disposal are more limited than the sets discussed in *The Sound Pattern of English.*

A second observation about the system concerns what may be called its direction. The system put forward in *The Sound Pattern of English* is one which appears to focus on how meaning is encoded into sound, in spite of the claims to neutrality between speaker and hearer which Chomsky and Halle have made repeatedly. They point out that an awareness of surface structure is necessary if one is to assign certain stress patterns correctly and to make the rules operate properly in the production of sentences. However, the task which confronts a reader is one of decoding print to discover meaning. His task is one of somehow getting to meaning through print. The beginning reader must use the visual cues he has on the page to reconstruct the meaning. He must somehow give a syntactic reading

to a phrase such as *American history teacher* (*[American history]
teacher* or *American [history teacher]*) before he can pronounce it
correctly. The writing system does not mark surface structure except
in certain gross ways, such as by word spacing and punctuation
marks. The beginning reader's task is apparently one of relating
symbols to sounds at an age when such abilities as that of assigning a
surface structure may be quite different from those of sophisticated
adults. Chomsky and Halle comment as follows on some of the
problems:

> There are many interesting questions that can be raised about the
> development of systems of underlying representation during the period of
> language acquisition. It is possible that this might be fairly slow. There is, for
> example, some evidence that children tend to hear much more phonetically
> than adults. There is no reason to jump to the conclusion that this is simply a
> matter of training and experience: it may very well have a maturational basis.
> Furthermore, much of the evidence relevant to the construction of the
> underlying systems of representation may not be available in early stages of
> language acquisition. These are open questions, and it is pointless to speculate
> about them any further. They deserve careful empirical study, not only
> because of the fundamental importance of the question of "psychological
> reality" of linguistic constructs, but also for practical reasons; for example,
> with respect to the problem of the teaching of reading (p.50).

The comment is most interesting because if empirical evidence
confirms the suspicion that Chomsky and Halle have, then it would
tend to justify much of the approach taken to reading by Bloomfield
and Fries. It would justify an approach which utilizes a taxonomic
phonemic, or broad phonetic, level of representation, which relates
such a level to orthographic patterns, and which excludes work with
derivational patterning in favor of work with sound-letter
associations. By some kind of happy default, such an approach does
not get itself involved with patterns of stress assignment in
polysyllabic works, patterns which one can assume a six-year old
already controls to a great extent by virtue of the fact that he is a
native speaker.

It could well be that the basic problem a child has in learning to
read is really one of learning the association between written symbols
and surface rather than deep phonology. For example, he must learn
that *hatter: hater, petter:Peter, dinner:diner; comma:coma,* and
supper:super show a systematic spelling difference associated with a
systematic surface phonological difference. In the terminology used
by reading teachers, he must learn that a double consonant indicates

a "short" vowel and that a single consonant plus vowel indicates a "long" vowel. Even though the use of the letters *a, e, i, o*, and *u* in the above words is "correct" in Chomsky and Halle's terms in spite of the very different phonetic realizations, the child's problem is one of cueing in the visual task involved in decoding, a task which even the generative-transformationalists refer to as the problem of identifying the visual response. Likewise, with a set of words like *metal, rebel, civil, Mongol*, and *cherub*, it is important that the child have available to him a strategy for approaching these words so that he can attempt to pronounce them as *metal* or *meetal, rebel* or *reeble*, and so on. It helps him very little to be told that the spellings are the best ones for English because there are also English words like *metallic, rebellion, civilian, Mongolian*, and *cherubic*. A six-year old is even less likely to know these derivatives than the base forms, and any knowledge about the "best" spellings for the second vowel in each word is more appropriate to teaching him to spell than to read. Perhaps *The Sound Pattern of English* is a better book for those interested in teaching spelling than in teaching reading, tasks which appear to be rather different!

What a child basically needs in beginning reading is a set of strategies for decoding print. No one is really sure what strategies successful beginning readers do employ. There is some reason to suspect that they do not use the strategies which teachers who believe in the various phonics approaches attempt to teach. These latter strategies, sometimes called phonic generalizations, have been severely attacked by linguists. However, a few of them seem to contain germs of truth, particularly recognizable after reading *The Sound Pattern of English*, as, for example, statements about final *e*'s making preceding vowels "long," about an *i* before *gh* having its "long" sound, about *c*'s before *e*'s or *i*'s being "soft," and so on. But then such is likely to be the case. Phonics instruction cannot be all wrong—rather it shows evidence of considerable confusion in its general orientation and the need for a transfusion of linguistic insights.

CONCLUSION

This discussion of the work of Bloomfield, Fries, Venezky, and Chomsky and Halle leads to certain conclusions. The first is that some linguists do have an interest in applying their theoretical knowledge to the solution of practical problems. However, the second is that the proposed applications vary considerably and the results are sometimes contradictory. Linguists have different ideas about linguistics and about the nature of the problems to which linguistics might contribute a solution. Some linguists are also more prescriptive in their proposals than others. It is possible to contrast the attempt by Fries at what appears to be a definitive attack on the reading problem to the extremely tentative suggestions put forward by Chomsky and Halle. Furthermore, the reading process itself is not an easy one to understand. Linguists have different notions about what language is, about how it may be described, about what its fundamental units are, about how these are related, and about what processes may operate. All these are linguistic matters quite properly and all have some relevance to understanding the reading process and teaching reading. But there are also non-linguistic matters which must be taken into account in considering problems in learning and teaching, and help must be sought from psychologists and educators as well as from linguists. The greatest need at present is for empirical work in which linguists, psychologists, and educators combine their insights in an attempt to improve our understanding of the reading process and of the teaching of reading.

chapter five
Research in Linguistics and Reading

The history of reading instruction is not very glorious if the interpretations by Diack (1965), Mathews (1966), and Chall (1967) are to be accepted. These critics show it to be a history filled with research studies that contradict one another, with gimmicks that have come and gone in regular cycles, and with sometimes bitter controversies over methods. It is not difficult to see the history as one in which claims about kinesthetics, tachistoscopes, phonic word-attack skills, reading pacers, whole-word methods, and bibliotherapy are advanced in one big, buzzing, babbling confusion. And, recently, claims about linguistics have been added to the clamor because linguistics is in fashion today among researchers in reading. But what kind of linguistic knowledge has found its way into reading instruction, both in materials and methods?

At the very beginning, we should observe that the linguistic knowledge which has found its way into reading is neither current linguistic knowledge nor very sound knowledge, either linguistically or pedagogically. It is necessary to attempt an evaluation of both the claims that have been made about the use of linguistics in reading and the experimental evidence that has been produced to date. These claims are extremely doubtful in most cases, and any experimental evidence that exists for the use of linguistics in reading is on the whole quite inadequate. As we have previously indicated, there can be no *linguistic* method for teaching reading, but linguistic knowledge properly applied to the teaching of reading should lead to improvements in such teaching. These improvements, however, can take place only if linguists cease to dabble in reading instruction and reading experts in linguistics. Both groups must become more serious about the others' problems and difficulties than they are at present. For example, most of the research carried out to prove or disprove the linguistic method of teaching reading accepts the views of such writers as Bloomfield and Barnhart (1961) and Fries (1963) as comprising such a method and questions neither the validity of the linguistic theories which these views reflect nor the argument that a good technique to use in linguistic analysis or linguistic presentation is therefore a good technique for reading instruction.

RESEARCH ON PHONEME-GRAPHEME CORRESPONDENCES

An examination of the texts which employ the linguistic method of teaching reading and of the research studies produced to date reveals that this method of teaching reading is extremely narrow. In essence, the linguistic method is little more than the presentation of regular phoneme-grapheme, or sound-spelling, relationships in beginning reading texts—a kind of phonics with a good dose of linguistic common sense added. The materials developed by the followers of Bloomfield and Fries reflect this concern and give virtually no indication that the possible linguistic contribution to reading involves anything more than the systematic introduction of the regularities and irregularities of English spelling. There is, in fact, scarcely more than an occasional passing reference to any other point that linguists have made about English.

What does the research based on the use of such materials reveal? First of all, the anecdotal evidence of such reports as that by Wilson and Lindsay (1963), with its account of the use of the Bloomfield materials for remedial work with 13 seventh graders reading at or below second grade level, must be discounted just as must be the "house organ" promotional studies of publishing companies. Fairly objective studies preferably involving nonremedial readers participating in replicable experiments, are what is required, and several such studies are worthy of mention. Wohleber (1953) compared the use of a set of Bloomfield's materials and the use of a set of basal materials with over 200 matched pairs of students for three years in classes moving from first to third grade. Significant differences favoring the Bloomfield materials were reported for all three grades. Sister Fidelia (1959) compared the Bloomfield approach with a phonics approach in a study involving first graders and found no significant differences in performance at the end of a year. Davis (1964) used modified Bloomfield materials to supplement a basal set of materials and compared this treatment with the use of basal materials alone in four groups of 23 first graders for one year. His results favored the combination, and his replication of the study with twelve groups confirmed his earlier results. Sheldon and Lashinger (1966), in a study using 21 randomly-assigned first grade classes over a one-year period, compared basal readers, modified linguistic materials, and linguistic readers but found scarcely any significant differences at all. An examination of these results leads to the conclusion that there is little evidence in favor of a linguistic method of teaching reading.

There are, however, two better studies than the studies just mentioned, those by Schneyer (1967) and Dolan (1966). These studies are much better documented and are on a much larger scale than the others. They are also very interesting because the linguistic method does not show up very well in either study. More important still, the studies also show how narrow that method is and how almost any method can be said to be *linguistic* if the investigator is bold enough to make such a claim.

Schneyer's research used two dozen first grade classes with twelve classes assigned to each of two treatment groups. One treatment group used an experimental edition of the Fries *Merrill Linguistic Readers* followed by the McKee *Reading for Meaning Series* while the other treatment group used the Robinson and Artley *The New Basic Readers*. Each treatment group was subdivided into three ability levels with four classes at each ability level. The classes, the teachers, and the treatments were all randomly assigned. The experiment was continued into the second grade with the loss of two classes, one from each treatment group. Here is Schneyer's conclusion at the end of the second grade, following the giving of a battery of tests to all pupils or to random samples of pupils:

> At the end of the second year of this three-year investigation, the major conclusion is that when the two treatment groups are considered as a whole neither of the two reading approaches produced significantly higher spelling or reading achievement that was consistent at all ability levels. While the basal reader treatment group obtained significantly higher total mean scores on four out of fourteen criterion variables, there was no significant difference between total treatment means for the remaining ten criteria. Three of the significant differences were on the Stanford Test given to all pupils in the study (subtests for Paragraph Meaning, Word Study Skills, and Spelling). The remaining criterion on which there was a significant difference between total means was the Accuracy score on the Gilmore Oral Reading Test that was obtained from the subsamples from each of the treatment groups (p.710).

The conclusion is that the linguistic method is neither better nor worse than the other method. Schneyer does report considerable interaction between treatment and ability level, so that with particular subgroups one treatment, not always the same one, is better than the other. However, what is abundantly clear from the study as a whole is the lack of any clearly significant superiority of one treatment over the other. In fact, the weight of the nonsignificant evidence actually favors the basal treatment, not the linguistic treatment.

In Dolan's study just over 400 fourth grade students in Detroit were matched with the same number of students in Dubuque for intelligence, sex, age, and socioeconomic status in an attempt to evaluate the beginning-reading programs of the two cities. Dolan characterized the differences between the reading programs in the two cities as follows:

> . . .it can be stated that the reading programs of the Dubuque and the Detroit systems differ radically in their basic concepts of reading in the initial stages. Dubuque schools emphasize the aspect of meaning from the first days of instruction. Word perception skills are built from a basic, meaningful sight vocabulary. Detroit schools assume with linguists that early mastery of the mechanics of word recognition is essential if the child is to develop the art of reading. It is only after he had learned how to get sounds from the printed page that the child can understand the meaning of these sounds (p.52).

In Dolan's opinion the children who formed the experimental group had obviously been taught by the linguistic method. However, her description of that method makes it sound more like a poor phonics program than a good linguistic program. Her conclusion is resoundingly in favor of the Detroit group.

> Although both samples performed above the national norms on all reading tests, the boys and girls of the experimental group recognized words in isolation more readily, used context with greater facility, had fewer orientation problems, possessed greater ability to analyze words visually, and had greater phonetic knowledge than boys and girls taught with the control method. There was no significant difference between the two samples in their ability to synthesize words.
>
> The boys and girls in the experimental group read faster and more accurately, had larger vocabularies, comprehended better, and were more able to retain factual information than the boys and girls in the control group. However, when the more complex comprehension abilities of organization and appreciation were examined, no significant differences were found between the two groups (p.63).

In spite of all this evidence, however, Dolan cannot quite bring herself to say that it is the method which is to be given the credit. This hesitation is welcome, for, if this is the linguistic method of teaching reading, it must really disturb a linguist. Even Barnhart himself (1967) does not consider this test a fair one, and says as much in a review of Dolan's report.

MODIFIED ALPHABETS

In any discussion of the linguistic method and its effectiveness reference must be made to modified alphabets since these are linguistic in nature. Such a modification as Unifon, as described by Malone (1962), deserves few words. Unifon is based on a poor understanding of English phonology and on the pedagogical principle that a difficult task should be made more difficult by denying a child the use of anything he might already have mastered of English orthography when he comes to school in favor of treating him like some kind of automatic scanning device.

In marked contrast to Unifon, the Initial Teaching Alphabet, or i.t.a., is an interesting modification of English orthographic patterns. It meets some of Bloomfield's and Fries' objections; it is based on a recognition of certain perceptual characteristics exhibited by successful readers; it is "method-free," being usable with any kind of teaching method; and it has its enthusiastic band of propagandizers. Linguistically, it is sound in some places and completely *ad hoc* in others.

What research evidence exists to support the use of i.t.a. in teaching beginning reading? Mazurkiewicz (1964, 1966) claims success in using i.t.a. for purposes of "phasing-in" beginning readers in experiments filled with uncontrolled variables. On the other hand, Fry (1966) reports evidence from a study employing a diacritical marking system, i.t.a., and a basal reading series in 21 first grade rooms that leads him to conclude that at the end of a year there were few differences among the three groups. More recently, Fry (1967) has written that:

> The weight of research seems to be leaning towards the conclusion that there is very little difference between the reading abilities of children taught in TO or i/t/a (p.553).

Like so much of the evidence in reading, the evidence for and against i.t.a. tends to be presented by partisans of one group or the other. Southgate's conclusion (1966), following a review of the research, is that there is a considerable Hawthorne effect present in the studies because of the publicity being given to i.t.a., and Downing himself (Downing, Cartwright, Jones, and Latham, 1967) has acknowledged the validity of some of Southgate's criticisms and answered only a few.

STUDIES OF SYNTAX

In spite of Lefevre's insistence (1964) on the importance of syntactic and intonational patterns in reading, there are only two good studies, both by Ruddell (1965, 1966), on this aspect of the use of linguistics in reading instruction. In the first of these studies, Ruddell devised six reading passages of 254 words each to investigate the following two hypotheses:

1. The degree of comprehension with which written passages are read is a function of the similarity of the written patterns of language structure to oral patterns of language structure used by children.

2. The comprehension scores on reading passages that utilize high frequency patterns of oral language structure will be significantly greater than the comprehension scores on reading passages that utilize low frequency patterns of oral language structure (p.404).

His study was conducted in the fourth grade, so he based his selection of patterns on descriptions of the language of fourth graders and controlled vocabulary differences, sentence lengths, and content. Using the cloze procedure and deleting every fifth word, he analyzed the data gathered from 131 subjects and found significant support for both hypotheses. However, since he also found intelligence, father's occupational status, parental educational level, and mental and chronological age related significantly to comprehension of the materials he devised, there are obviously many other important variables in addition to linguistic ones. In fact, among those differences Ruddell took into account, it is rather surprising to find that only sex differences were not significant.

In the second report, Ruddell describes his progress in a longitudinal study devoted to determining how the use of greater or lesser amounts of phoneme-grapheme correspondences and controlled sentence patterns affects reading ability in two dozen first grade classrooms. He reports finding evidence, some significant and some not, for his hypothesis that these variables are important.

These studies by Ruddell are important studies, but again they touch on only certain linguistic matters and they hardly touch at all on those matters that concern current linguistic researchers. In fact, it would be true to say that very few researchers in reading are really up-to-date with what is happening currently in linguistics.

All the studies reported here are inconclusive, possibly for three main reasons. The first is that the view of linguistics incorporated into materials for the so-called *linguistic* method is not a very insightful one. The second is that the methods used by linguists are not methods for teaching reading but methods for doing linguistics. The third is that teachers using linguistic materials apparently use them in the same old ways and make no more than token gestures toward linguistics. And when they do make such gestures, they are toward a linguistics which is not current linguistics.

CURRENT LINGUISTICS

The important dimension that is missing from the work that has been done so far in applying linguistic knowledge to reading instruction is the linguistic knowledge acquired over the past decade. The kind of linguistics which is partially introduced into some versions of the linguistic method is Bloomfieldian linguistics; however, beginning with the publication of Chomsky's *Syntactic Structures* (1957), linguistics has undergone a revolution. It would not be fair to say that Bloomfieldian linguistics is dead or even moribund, but it has been largely superseded by generative-transformational linguistics.

Generative-transformational linguists make a distinction between the skills and competence a person must have to behave linguistically and his actual observed linguistic behavior. The first interests them much more than the second. They also try to account for the first in a highly formalized way by writing precise rules. Furthermore, generative-transformationalists are unwilling to separate phonology from grammar as the Bloomfieldians tried to do, and they seek to include the study of meaning in their study of language, not to exclude it. There are undoubtedly some direct consequences for reading instruction in such concerns as these, but on the whole generative-transformationalists have been reluctant to hypothesize what these might be. However, a few may be mentioned.

First, it is impossible to separate syntax and phonology or syntax and spelling because they are closely interrelated. It is not necessary to postulate a phonemic level of linguistic organization in the Bloomfield or Fries sense, so any overinsistence on phoneme-grapheme correspondences is likely to be misplaced. Linguistic behavior itself is rule-governed, but these rules are extremely abstract and subconscious; they must be deduced rather than induced. In order to study the process of comprehension it is necessary to know what has to be comprehended (that is the actual linguistic content of any sentence) and to know what rule-governed processes enter into comprehension (that is how that content is processed). Even mistakes should be thought of as applications of the wrong rules, as evidences of faulty processing, rather than as instances of random behavior.

A growing body of experimental evidence exists to support such claims. Some recent papers and summaries may be mentioned. Wardhaugh (1968, 1969) has pointed out some changes in emphasis that current linguistics would demand of investigations in reading. Goodman and his fellow workers (1967) have begun a systematic series of studies of what Goodman calls "miscues" in reading, and Weaver (1967) and Weaver and Kingston (1967) have marshalled some very interesting evidence to suggest that what is currently happening in linguistics will lead to a complete revolution in our thinking about the applications of linguistics to reading. Weaver suggests that:

> ...there is an apparent contradiction in the attitude of the teacher toward the word as a unit of language and that of the linguist and certain psychologists who base their experiments on the logical analyses of the linguists (p.267).

One can add that four of the linguistic units that teachers apparently find it extremely easy to talk about and even to define—sound, syllable, word, and sentence—create great problems of definition for linguists. It is even possible to say that linguistics is all about finding suitable definitions for these terms. In this connection Weaver and Kingston conclude by saying that "the linguist is talking about things which the teacher of reading needs to know" (p.242). Studies such as those by Marks (1967) and Mehler and Carey (1967) offer further confirmation of claims made by others on such matters as the importance of deep structure.

CONCLUSION

Since linguists are concerned with such matters as those just mentioned, there is *no* linguistic approach to the teaching of reading at the moment and, very definitely, no linguistic method. It is doubtful that there can be a linguistic method or even a linguistic approach. However, there might be a linguistic perspective, some kind of basic knowledge which can be applied to reading instruction (Wardhaugh, 1969). Obviously, too, there are methods and techniques which teachers would not employ in teaching reading if they had more linguistic knowledge, and knowing what not to do and what to avoid seem to be essential prerequisites to knowing what to do.

What is known as the linguistic method is neither very good linguistics nor very good method, and what success there has been was derived as much from Hawthorne effects as from the linguistic insights found in the materials used. However, there is a great demand for better content in reading instruction: phonics methods still continue to be based on quite inadequate notions about language, and look-and-say methods and other methods which stress meaning continue to be based on vague notions of syntax and semantics. Teachers of reading need an awareness of current linguistic ideas and a greater familiarity with the linguistic content of reading. Reading is basically a language process. Linguistics is the study of language. Adequate methods for teaching reading should be based in part on the best existing knowledge of language and linguistics. To that extent linguistics will be invaluable in teaching reading. However, serious doubt exists that the use of linguistic knowledge in reading instruction will ever add up to a linguistic method of teaching reading.

chapter six
Phonics and Comprehension

An examination of the literature on reading instruction suggests two major emphases: one is on reading as the decoding of written symbols, with a resulting concern for orthography, and the other is on reading for meaning, with a resulting concern for mental processes of a fairly high order. The distinction is between emphasis on the code and emphasis on the message. When the reading researcher or reading teacher places emphasis on the code, there is likely to be a concentration on phonics, phoneme-grapheme correspondences, possible improvements of the existing orthography, and using oral reading as part of the teaching process. On the other hand, an emphasis on the message leads to a concentration on look-and-say techniques, the importance of meaningful content, and the avoidance of oral reading in favor of silent reading.

In practice, most teachers seem to emphasize both code and message in varying proportions although at times certain experts have come out strongly in favor of one emphasis to the apparent exclusion of the other. In teaching reading, it is necessary to recognize both code and message, both the fact that in some sense the written language is a codification of the spoken language (that is that the orthography is important) and the fact that the code is used for meaningful communication and that rather complex types of processing are required. In order to teach beginning reading successfully, teachers should employ methods based on adequate notions of the relationship of sound and symbol in the first case and what has to be comprehended in the second. In general, existing methods are based on notions which are far from adequate: phonics instruction, the decoding emphasis, is a mishmash of fact and fiction; and the prevailing understanding of comprehension, the message emphasis, derives more from mystical than scientific sources of inspiration.

At this time the reading process itself need not be defined any more closely than in the preceding paragraph. If that definition seems inadequate, few apologies are needed. Most definitions are much less adequate because they are too vague (reading as getting meaning from the printed page), or too all-inclusive (reading as a psycho-neuromuscular-socioeconomically correlated activity), or too utopian (reading as the key to better living in a better world filled with better people), or too narrow (reading as barking at print or reading as high-speed recognition). Only two claims will be made. The first is that no matter what else a definition of reading includes, it must recognize that a connection exists between English orthography and the phonological system of English. The second is that sentences have meanings that can be accounted for in terms of syntactic and semantic rules. The first of these claims will be discussed in connection with the teaching of phonics and the second in connection with the teaching of comprehension.

PHONICS INSTRUCTION

Within the last decade three books have appeared which contained strongly phrased and quite similar conclusions. The first, Hunter Diack's *The Teaching of Reading in Spite of the Alphabet* (1965), criticizes the reading research of the twentieth century on the grounds that it has discovered very little of consequence. Diack concludes that a satisfactory method for teaching reading would have to be based on a recognition of the alphabetic nature of English and would, to that extent, be a phonics method. Mitford Mathews, in his *Teaching to Read: Historically Considered* (1966) is also critical of reading research and phonics, or the synthetic plan as he calls it, claiming that any objective research that has been done clearly favors that approach:

> The fact is well established that children taught by a carefully worked out synthetic plan read much better and read sooner than those taught by an analytic method, or by any combination of approaches in which the analytic element predominates. The evidence for this statement is abundant and is constantly being augmented (p.196).

More recently, Jeanne Chall, in *Learning to Read: The Great Debate* (1967), written following a three-year study financed by the Carnegie Corporation, pronounces in favor of a phonics approach in the teaching of beginning reading, although not quite as definitely as either of the other two and with considerably more restraint in her method of argument.

All three authors make similar points: valid research evidence to support look-and-say and other whole-word methods over phonics methods does not exist and fair comparisons nearly always show phonics instruction to result in the development of superior reading achievement. This conclusion does not surprise a linguist, for it seems quite obvious that such would be the case—that a method which shows children who are learning to read the relationship between sounds and symbols is more likely to be successful in teaching beginning reading than other methods which almost entirely ignore that relationship. However, when the same linguist looks at what is taught in phonics, he generally cannot help but be disturbed, for it appears that if existing phonics methods are better than other methods in teaching beginning reading, a phonics method based on linguistically defensible information would produce even more startling results. If the present phonics programs do succeed, either they succeed at high cost or else their success is more a testimony to the children who learned to read *in spite of* the phonics instruction rather than as a result of it.

Some familiar books and articles on phonics are worth a little examination. Roma Gans' *Fact and Fiction about Phonics* (1964) really contains more fiction than fact, for Gans finds considerable difficulty distinguishing one from the other. She has no conception of how language functions or how language is learned, and she has no ability to keep statements about sounds quite clearly differentiated from those about symbols. The book contains a completely uncritical treatment of the notion of "long" and "short" vowels and of syllabication; there is confusion about phonetic facts and the sound-spelling relationship; and throughout Gans fails to distinguish statements about the intuitive knowledge people, including children, have about their language from those about conscious knowledge, that is the knowledge they can verbalize. The book is almost valueless, and its title is most unfortunate. Somewhat better is Arthur Heilman's *Phonics in Proper Perspective* (1964), but it contains several of the same misunderstandings. A third book, Anna Cordts' *Phonics for the Reading Teacher* (1965), is still better, for it contains less confusion and much more common sense about language. Of course, there are unfortunate normative statements about correctness, and the notion of separating out the individual sounds of words, particularly final consonants which in normal speech tend to be very weakly articulated, for the purpose of sounding-out exercises is extremely ill-advised. However, on the whole, the book far surpasses either of the two. The best book is Delores Durkin's *Phonics and the Teaching of Reading* (1965). On the whole though books on phonics are not very distinguished.

These comments have, in effect, been a general condemnation of phonics instruction as represented in texts. What is being condemned are statements of the following kinds because each is linguistically indefensible:

1. Statements about letters having sounds: for example, "these letters must be blended to arrive at the correct sound." Letters are letters and sounds are sounds; they must not be confused with each other.

2. Statements about syllabication which apply only to word-breaking conventions in printing when these statements are made into rules of pronunciation: for example, *butter* is broken into *but* and *ter* and *monkey* into *mon* and *key*. There is only one medial consonant in *butter*, and its phonetic quality derives from its relationship to both vowels in the word, not just from its relationship to the first vowel.

3. Statements about slurring, poor enunciation, incorrect articulation, and mispronunciations: for example, *doing* is said to be "incorrectly" pronounced if said as *doin'*. A set of such shibboleths exists.

4. Statements about "long" and "short" vowels: for example, *mad* is said to have a short vowel and *mate* a long vowel, even though in every dialect of English the second vowel is shorter in duration than the first. Allophonic vowel length depends on whether the vowel is final or non-final in a word or whether it is followed by a voiced or voiceless consonant. There are phonetically "long" and "short" vowels in English, but these are something quite different from the "long" and "short" vowels described in books on reading.

5. Statements about teaching children the sounds of their language as though they did not already know these. They could not speak if they did not *know* the sounds of their language.

6. Statements which do not allow for well-known dialect variations: for example, *when* is nearly always taught as /hwen/ no matter which part of the United States the child comes from, or *due* as /dyuw/, or *pin* and *pen* must be differentiated.

The preceding are just some of the readily observable weakenesses of the phonics instruction that according to Diack, Mathews, and Chall has proved to be *superior* to other kinds of instruction. It is a mixture of fact and fiction. Description and prescription go hand-in-hand, but the teacher apparently never knows which is which. Speech and writing are confused. The teaching of reading is associated with the teaching of some kind of proper speech, but the latter is never defined precisely. Worse still, there is more teaching about an artificial and haphazard set of observations, or generalizations, than teaching of the desired responses.

There are attempts to conduct serious research into the problems inherent in phonics instruction. Of course, given the nature of the phonics just described, lots of problems will exist, many of them created by the instruction itself. A series of articles by Clymer (1963), Bailey (1967), and Burmeister (1968) published in *The Reading Teacher* have shown how different investigators have researched "phonic generalizations." These investigators examined a set of statements which in many cases hardly require any examination at all. Some are valueless because they fly in the face of linguistic common sense: for example, "in many two- and three-syllable words the final *e* lengthens the vowel in the last syllable" —a confusion of sound and symbol; or "if the last syllable of a word ends in *le*, the consonant preceding the *le* usually begins the last syllable" —the blind acceptance of the so-called "rules of syllabication." Others obviously require ordering so that a statement such as "*r* gives the preceding vowel a sound that is neither long nor short" must precede the statement that "when a vowel is in the middle of a one-syllable word, the vowel is short." However, these two rules are not ordered, nor is ordering even considered. The generalizations seem to be a haphazard set in which rules about accent, word-splitting, silent letters, and special combinations are presented randomly and without motivation. Burmeister's conclusion that not many of them are very useful is hardly suprising, for no child could ever learn to read by applying a set of rules of this kind. It would have been more productive to have ordered the rules in some way, reduced their number considerably, and thrown out the obviously indefensible ones—or, better still, to have investigated *just which rules children actually do use* by studying their errors, or miscues in Goodman's terminology (1967), in word attack.

It is not surprising that several linguists who have turned their attention to the teaching of reading should have concentrated on phonics or something resembling phonics. Bloomfield was highly critical of existing phonics instruction. His position has been stated by Barnhart in his promotional literature for *Let's Read: A Linguistic Approach* (1961):

> A phonic system starts from the written language and teaches a child to learn to read as if he had never learned to talk. It asks him to produce isolated sounds and to combine them, which is a meaningless exercise that can only delay the child in learning to read.

The Bloomfield system is not phonics as phonics is usually described. There is no sounding out, and any interpretation which suggests that Bloomfield believed in sounding out (other than getting children to name the letters they see to insure that they can discriminate the letters) is completely false. Fries, in his *Linguistics and Reading* (1963), also opposed phonics instruction; in fact, he devoted the whole of this fifth chapter to the proper definition of three important terms: *phonics, phonetics,* and *phonemics*. This chapter should be required reading for all reading teachers. Like Bloomfield, Fries insisted on the recognition of whole words and was opposed to sounding out. Instead he stressed the contrast, oral and visual, of pairs of words such as *mat, met* and *fat, fate*. In both cases, the method has come to be known as a linguistic method rather than a phonics method although little reason can be found for this distinction except for purposes of differentiation. If children are to be taught to associate sounds and spellings, then such teaching has to be based on good descriptions of the sound and spelling systems of English and of their relationship. Bloomfield and Fries offer reasonably valid statements of this relationship, that is given certain assumptions of a kind rather different from those which many linguists accept today. They are not carried away with irrelevant issues about "long" and "short" vowels, syllable divisions, normative judgments, and so on. In addition, they propose some principles of gradation and contrast which might be useful and oppose others, such as "sounding out," which are very likely to be harmful. Their linguistic method is a variety of good phonics; other people's phonics is almost certainly very poor linguistics.

It is fortunate that today there is at least one reasonably sound approach available which goes some way to meeting the kind of objections Bloomfield and Fries had to phonics. This is the Initial Teaching Alphabet or i.t.a. Used by teachers who avoid the worst prescriptions of phonics, this alphabet has much to recommend it.

Certainly, it has its inconsistencies. Nevertheless, it is a rather laudable attempt to help children make some kind of sense out of English orthographic conventions in their attempt to learn to read—and that *is* phonics.

Anyone seriously interested in teaching children to read must be prepared to acquire a knowledge of the phonological system of English. He must also find out how that system is represented in English orthography; how people, particularly six-year-olds, actually speak; and how such speech varies in the different dimensions of social and regional dialects. He must also become aware that children know their language when they come to school (for they can speak), and that children bring grammatical and lexical knowledge as well as phonological knowledge to the task of reading. In one sense i.t.a. overdifferentiates since it ignores this latter fact, just as did Bloomfield and Fries. Actually, traditional phonics shows more awareness of the importance of root words and derivational patterning than do some of the linguists who have written about phoneme-grapheme correspondences. In other words, not all of phonics is bad. Fortunately, linguists today have realized some of the inadequacies of the notion of the phoneme held by earlier linguists such as Bloomfield and Fries and go so far as to claim that traditional English orthography is not at all a bad representation of English phonology. They also make the very interesting claim that it is useful regardless of dialect, so long as it is treated as a representation of important underlying contrasts and not as a representation of surface peculiarities.

Undoubtedly the best known analysis of English spelling patterns available to teachers is that by Venezky (1967). In this analysis, Venezky discusses the purely orthographic conventions such as the use of letters like *x* and *q*, combinations like *th* and *ch*, the predictable alternations between *u*'s and *w*'s and *i*'s and *y*'s, the basis for so-called long-short distinctions in pairs like *hater* and *hatter* and *diner* and *dinner*, and some of the other morphophonemic alternations in English, as in *sign* and *signal*, *bomb* and *bombadier*, and *autumn* and *autumnal*. Venezky's analysis is very much in keeping with current developments in linguistic thought and may be recommended to anyone who wants to put phonics onto a respectable basis.

COMPREHENSION

The process of comprehension is often characterized as one of gathering thought from the printed page or of fusing the meanings of words together generally in some cumulative linear fashion—whatever these notions mean. Buswell (1959), for example, writes that the unit in reading materials is the same as the unit in speech, namely, the word, and that reading is a process of fusing single words into sequences of meaning. Such notions are palpably inadequate. They rely too heavily on naive ideas about words. Words are important grammatical units in English, but they are not the same units in every case as those found in the dictionaries. Nor does one understand sentences by simply adding together the meanings of words. Such definitions about gathering thoughts and fusing meanings do not say anything interesting at all about the process of comprehension. Understanding the process of comprehension requires some idea of the components of sentences which are important in making sentences meaningful. Without a characterization of what is involved in comprehension, no very interesting statements can be made about comprehension. All one can talk about is success or failure measured in rather gross terms or types of error without precise specification of the sources of difficulty. Current linguistics does offer some understanding of the act of comprehension in that it has something to say about these components. It is not a complete understanding and has more to do with the fundamental syntactic and semantic relationships in sentences than with how these actually constitute functional units in any psychological process of comprehension.

In order to fully comprehend a sentence, a reader must be able to relate what many linguists call the deep structure of that sentence, that is its basic elements and their relationships, to its surface structure, that is the representation of that sentence on the printed page. The reader must also be able to project a consistent semantic reading on the individual words. He must do more than react to the surface structure of a sentence alone, that is he must do more than recognize individual letters, words, and superficial syntactic patterns. To do only this much is to bark at print. Genuine comprehension requires that each sentence be given both syntactic and semantic interpretations in depth. This process is an active one to which the reader makes a great contribution. It is by no means the passive process that certain linguists have claimed it is.

The following five sentences may be used in a somewhat oversimplified discussion to make some basic points:

1 The man stole the car.
2 The car was stolen.
3 Who stole the car?
4 What did the man steal?
5 What was stolen?

The first sentence requires that the reader understand that *The man* is the deep subject of the sentence of which *stole the car* is the predicate, and *the car* is the deep object. The second sentence has a surface subject *The car* but the real subject, the deep subject, is an unspecified SOMEONE. *The car* is actually what was stolen, so SOMEONE stole it and *the car* is still the deep object. The deep structure accounts for the fact that a correct interpretation of *The car was stolen* requires an understanding that an unspecified person did the stealing and that this person stole the car. The other sentences are understood as follows: Sentence 3 is a question about SOMEONE who stole the car and seeks the identity of that SOMEONE. Sentence 4 is also a question but this time seeks the identity of the stolen SOMETHING (we do not know what it is) and specifies who the guilty party was. We can contrast sentence 5 with sentence 4: in sentence 5 neither the guilty party nor what was stolen is specified.

These five sentences have been analyzed in an extremely simple way, but the principle is clear: in teaching comprehension one must understand exactly what must be comprehended. What must be comprehended is more that the meanings of the individual words in a sentence. A good part of what must be comprehended must be accounted for by a knowledge of the deep syntactic relationships in the sentences presented for comprehension. Another part of what must be comprehended can be accounted for if one has a parallel knowledge of the semantic readings that are possible. One can account in some systematic or principled way for the different readings of *play* in the following sentences:

6 He wrote a fine play.
7 He made a fine play.
8 The wheel has too much play.
9 All she does all day is play.

We can note the semantic relationships and/or constraints between *wrote* and *play* in sentence 6, between *made* and *play* in sentence 7, and between *wheel* and *play* in sentence 8. Sentence 9, on the other hand, seems neutral.

Current linguistic investigations promise some help in coming to a better understanding of what is involved in teaching comprehension than the understanding which presently exists. It must be emphasized once more that the descriptions of the syntactic and semantic systems which linguists offer are just that and no more. They are descriptions of linguistic abstractions and not of psychological processes. They do at least warn us against thinking of comprehension as some kind of mystical process which one has no hope of examining and against giving an unhealthy emphasis to individual words at the expense of other far more important units and processes.

CONCLUSION

Good materials·and methods for teaching reading should reflect good linguistic knowledge. Five principles for developing good materials and methods for teaching reading can be stated:

1. They must be based on sound linguistic content, that is on the best available description of language—and of the English language in particular—rather than on random collections of myths. Scientific knowledge is needed, not folklore. Linguists have such knowledge of English phonology, orthography, syntax, and semantics.

2. They must be based on a sound knowledge of the relationships and differences between sounds and symbols, and between speech and writing. Linguists recognize some basic dichotomies; reading teachers must also be aware of these dichotomies.

3. They must be based on a thorough understanding of just what children know about their language as this knowledge reveals itself in what they can do in their language rather than in what they can verbalize about their language. This distinction is extremely important but is hardly ever made in discussions of beginning reading. Six-year-olds are sophisticated users of the language. Very few of us can handle a foreign language with the same ease and assurance as first grade children handle English, even when these children are from culturally different environments.

4. They must differentiate between descriptive and prescriptive statements, particularly when the prescriptions are unrealistic. When the prescriptions refer to Standard English, the methods and materials should reflect some decision about the relationship (if any)

between teaching reading and teaching a standard spoken dialect. It may well be that Standard English orthography is quite adequate for teaching reading to speakers of *any* dialect of English.

5. Finally, they must recognize the important active contribution the learner makes in reading, both in trying to make sense of the orthographic conventions of English and in trying to make sense out of sentences. Too often the learner's correct responses are rewarded and his incorrect responses punished. Good methods and materials should focus on these incorrect responses, or "miscues," for they can tell just as much as one will let them tell; and they probably tell a great deal, for they are rarely quite random.

chapter seven
Syllabication

It is sometimes said that almost a full generation elapses before professionals put to use newly discovered knowledge and up to two generations elapse before that knowledge finds its way into the textbooks used in schools. Something of the truth of this statement can be seen in the treatment in course manuals, teacher texts, and school books of such topics as the sentence, the word, the syllable, and the letter. In the majority of school books sentences are still defined as groups of words which make sense though some very recent books do refer to the importance of sentence patterns and intonation. Neither teachers nor authors appear to be greatly interested in what constitutes a word since they assume that readily available dictionaries have solved that problem. Finally, children are still instructed to pronounce letters correctly and led through the ritual of working out the syllables in English words so that they may either spell better, read better, or write better.

Just as some of the difficulties in teaching children to write better sentences or use words more skillfully arise from a lack of knowledge on the teacher's part of what sentences and words might be, so some of the confusion about the nature and the status of the syllable and the processes and ideas involved in syllabication results from a similar lack of knowledge. In such circumstances teachers should know what linguists have had to say about English syllables.

SYLLABLES

Linguists are agreed that speech is usually produced in stretches of sound larger than the individual phonemes, which are the smallest individually significant sounds of a language. Using kymographic tracings, Stetson (1951) postulated that certain ballistic chest movements result in syllables, and most linguists are agreed that English speakers use certain characteristic chest pulses. For example, Gleason (1961) writes:

Speech is. . .marked by a series of short pulses produced by this motion of the intercostal muscles. These pulses are the phonetic *syllables* (p.258).

The critical word in this statement is *phonetic* and Gleason uses it deliberately since the significance in any language of the pulses themselves is open to question. Pike (1943) has also emphasized the same point:

> A *syllable* is a single unit of movement of the lung initiator . . . which includes but one crest of speed . . . . *Real syllables* are those which the ear is physiologically capable of distinguishing. *Perceptual syllables* are those which an investigator actually notices at some particular time (pp. 116-117).

The pulses, characterized in English by sonority according to Bloomfield (1933, p.120) and Jones (1957, p.56fn) or stressed peaks according to Hockett (1958, pp.99-100), do occur but the significance of their occurrence within the total language structure is not completely settled.

In some languages, for example French with its open syllable type, the syllable is obviously an important phonetic characteristic of the language and has to be taken into account in a thoroughgoing description of the significant structural units of the language. However, because English has no characteristic syllable type, the status of the syllable as a significant unit in the overall structure of the English language is somewhat uncertain.

Even if one is prepared to say that the syllable is a significant characteristic of English, several problems are still left unresolved. Although the number of syllables in an English utterance can be fairly easily determined, the precise point at which one syllable ends and another begins is often impossible to determine. In any language every sound is influenced by the sounds or silences which precede and follow it; therefore, a consonant sound between two vowels is influenced by both vowels. Such a consonant may be called an interlude and there is no exact "point of syllable division" (Hockett, 1955, p.52) in such an interlude; that is the consonant belongs as much to one vowel as the other. Jones (1957, pp.55-58) has pointed out that whereas syllable peaks are fairly easy to find in English, the syllable limits are impossible to define. The result is that the syllable divisions recorded in a written text are made according to convention and are essentially arbitrary.

SYLLABICATION

When English words are divided in writing according to their "syllables," the division points have little or no relevance to phonological facts. The actual division points have evolved mainly through many years of concern with proofreading, typesetting, laying out written words as attractively as possible, and breaking words at line ends. Such divisions have, therefore, no value for any other purpose, yet they are constantly referred to in spelling manuals, reading texts, and pronunciation guides as though they had a much wider applications. Even when a good dictionary does explain what syllable division means, most users of the dictionary still seem to persist in ignoring or misusing the information. The editors of *Webster's Third New International Dictionary* for example, go to great pains to explain the rationale of their syllable division in the orthography of each word and they do not mark syllable divisions in pronunciation. However, authors of school books of all kinds still persist in confusing orthography and pronunciation.

It is even true to say that many authors are prepared to write quite boldly about syllables and syllable division without ever defining their terms or without being aware of the problems with which they are dealing. A typical statement is as follows:

The children should be taught the meaning of the word *syllable*. . . . There are as many syllables as there are *pronounced* vowels (Hildreth, 1955, p.233).

Such a circular statement is scarcely better than no statement at all, particularly as most children and most of their teachers seem to believe that the vowel sounds of English number five—or sometimes six or seven. Still other writers try to differentiate between "sound" syllables and "sight" syllables, and even go so far as to point out the conventions implicit in the latter classification. The results, however, are quite often unsatisfactory. For example, this same text states that:

Expert spellers invariably pronounce and spell by syllables when dealing with the longer, regularly formed words (p.233).

Fortunately for such spellers, the statement is not correct and its very inadequacy can be demonstrated by examining the rules for syllabication which follow the statement, rules in which phonological, morphological, and orthographic criteria are haphazardly interwoven.

It is not only in books on spelling that such agglomerations of rules can be found: books on reading are just as prone to confusion. One can only wonder at the possible results of an exercise such as the following taken from a reading manual:

> To illustrate the method of dividing words with double consonants into syllables, write on the chalkboard the following words . . . *mittens supper*. . .
>
> Ask the children to pronounce each word and tell how many syllables they hear. Have volunteers...show where the second syllable begins in each word....After all the words have been divided correctly, help the children to state the principle: *When double consonants come between two vowels in a word, the word is divided between the consonants* (Russell and Wulfing, 1955, p.142).

The weakness of the attempted connection between the symbols and the sounds can be easily demonstrated. A pronunciation of *mittens* which followed the rules for syllabication in writing would be /mĭt + ténz/, whereas a normal pronunciation is /mit ənz/. The differences in allophones, junctures, phonemes, stresses, and morphological structure are readily apparent.

Perhaps the most alarming feature of so many of the· statements made about syllabication is a seeming insistence on truth. When one sees reading texts in which the authors give "words correctly analyzed into syllables" as follows: *mon-key, but-ter, pump-kin, kan-ga-roo*, and *chrys-an-the-mum*, he can only wonder that children ever succeed in reading at all and should not be surprised that certain children have great difficulty in "blending sounds and syllables." The really surprising fact is that so many children actually do succeed rather than that so few do not.

Still other texts suggest exercises in which words are presented and pronounced syllable by syllable. The actual stresses in such words are completely ignored. Other exercises suggest that the syllables will often be well-known smaller words:

> When this is the case, syllabification tends to reinforce the dependence upon the technique of known words within larger words. For example *dam age* is separated into two usable words (Bond and Wagner, 1960, p. 183).

Again, phonological facts, stress, meaning, and even elementary common sense seem to be completely dispensable.

CONCLUSION

Certain basic points about syllabication emerge from the preceding discussion:

1. It is very likely that there are significant syllable units in English speech and that these units are characterized by their vowel peaks.

2. Syllables flow into each other. Because syllable boundaries overlap, consonants between syllables, particularly single consonants, may belong to both syllables.

3. English spelling is not simply a representation of English sounds, and English writing conventions are quite often based on considerations that have nothing to do with sounds at all.

4. Syllabication has no "truth" value. It has, however, some pragmatic value in that it is a further way of encouraging students to learn to spell, to read, or to conform to English writing conventions.

5. Dictionary syllabication has almost nothing to do with phonology and almost everything to do with the conventions of a writing system.

6. Exercises which require students to say how many syllables a word has have some value; exercises which insist that students decide where syllables really begin and end cannot be justified on linguistic grounds.

7. If the use of hyphens at line ends is worth teaching, it should be taught from a good dictionary; however, even good dictionaries sometimes disagree with each other in particular cases.

8. Polysyllabic words may be broken down phonologically, morphologically, visually, and typographically. In any particular analysis of such a word the analyst should state which principle he is using and his reasons for using that principle.

chapter eight
Language Acquisition and Reading

Numerous summaries of research in language acquisition exist: McCarthy (1954) summarizes work completed prior to 1950; Elkonin (1958), Brown and Berko (1960), Carroll (1960), Brown (1965), Ervin-Tripp (1966), Ervin-Tripp and Slobin (1966), McNeill (1966, 1970a, 1970b), and Slobin (1971) summarize parts, or the whole, of more recent work; and Kelley (1967) provides one of the most interesting discussions of many of the major issues. The purpose of this chapter is to isolate and assess major theories of language acquisition and to relate these theories to beginning reading instruction. The particular focus is the acquisition of syntax. The theories are also reviewed only from the perspective of the linguistic knowledge available today; consequently, little attention is given to important cognitive and affective factors. These factors should not be considered unimportant in beginning reading instruction; rather, they are beyond the scope of the chapter.

ATHEORETICAL STUDIES

A reading of McCarthy's summary article (1954) induces mixed feelings in a linguist. She reports on a wide variety of descriptive and normative studies, but all seem unrevealing insofar as current interests in language acquisition are concerned. The studies reported appear atheoretical today because the investigators made little attempt to formulate and test fruitful hypotheses and to handle data other than quantitatively. Consequently, no coherent account of language acquisition emerges from the studies reviewed by McCarthy. Instead, child language appears to drift somehow from a prevocalic stage, through various stages replete with errors and deficiencies, toward the clearly articulated speech of an ideal speaker of Standard English. As a result, sounds "emerge" in ways that are never specified, "first words" are uttered at a characteristic time, grammatical distinctions are "acquired," often through the elimination of various "errors," and vocabularies "expand" as the child's dictionary gains more entries. Gradually, by some process of successive approximation, the child's language becomes more and more like the language ascribed in traditional grammars to those who speak the language "properly."

Working in such a way, investigators may try to discover when the child learns to distinguish *pin* from *pen* and *witch* from *which*, all the while ignoring the fact that in certain dialects such distinctions are not made at all. Or they may try to count various sentence types using formulas for sentence description that derive from analyses of writing and studies of rhetorical devices rather than from any close observation of spoken language. Or they may calculate word frequencies and compute type-token ratios without defining the concept of "a word" or devising the most appropriate elicitation procedures. Such investigators often collect considerable quantities of data which can be neatly inventoried and displayed in tables and figures (for example, tables of errors in articulation which show a gradual reduction in frequency as age increases). However, the data are essentially unrevealing because the investigators do not ask why it is that one linguistic skill is acquired before another, or what is the nature of the linguistic ability of the child at various stages in his linguistic development.

Only in recent years have such questions been asked by psychologists and linguists engaged in the study of language acquisition. They have realized that inventories are unrevealing unless they show which items contrast with each other within the inventories. They no longer disregard regional and social variations in speech and developments in modern linguistics. They also insist that it is impossible to describe language acquisition without first spelling out either a specific theory of language or a general theory of learning. Therefore, recent work on language acquisition confronts these theoretical issues. It does so at the expense of large-scale data collection, investigators preferring to test out hypotheses on as few as two or three children, as Brown and Bellugi (1964) did with Adam and Eve, or on a single phonological, grammatical, or semantic distinction, as Klima and Bellugi (1966) did with negation.

One issue that has never been dealt with satisfactorily, even in recent work, is the specification of the ultimate linguistic knowledge or ability that is being acquired. Obviously, more is involved than knowledge of a dictionary or of an inventory of sentence patterns, or the ability to combine words and patterns. N. Chomsky (1965) has proposed the term *competence*, as distinguished from *performance*, to describe this knowledge. However, this term has become more of a slogan than a well-defined concept in linguistics. Since research in language acquisition must focus on such issues as "increasing complexity" and "developing competence," a certain vagueness results when the end point toward which the child is assumed to be progressing still remains largely hidden from view. Menyuk (1969) discusses some of the problems that result in attempts to interpret data in such circumstances. Fortunately, many of the data are not in dispute among those who study language acquisition, for all agree that certain stages or trends can be observed: babbling ends around 18 months; holophrastic utterances precede two- and three-word utterances; early speech is "telegraphic"; control of word order antedates control of inflections; and comprehension outstrips production. The interpretation of the data is the crucial issue.

BEHAVIORISTIC THEORIES

In his book *Verbal Behavior*, Skinner (1957) proposes a comprehensive theory of language acquisition and language behavior in which specific linguistic behaviors are acquired through operant conditioning and then extended through response generalization. The devastating review of the book by N. Chomsky (1959) demonstrates the inappropriateness of Skinner's proposal. Chomsky's criticisms reiterate earlier arguments from *Syntactic Structures* (1957) that existing theories of language are inadequate for almost any purpose and that the kind of theory he himself proposes is needed. The review also attacks the adequacy of reinforcement theory and the notion of generalization, as formulated by Skinner, in explaining either language acquisition or language behavior. Chomsky claims that the theory is illusionary, that most of its concepts are irrelevant in explaining linguistic behavior, and that the real issues are never confronted. Chomsky is particularly critical of Skinner's failure to recognize the contribution that the child makes to language acquisition, declaring that:

...a refusal to study the contribution of the child to language learning permits only a superficial account of language acquisition, with a vast and unanalyzed contribution attributed to a step called "generalization" which in fact, includes just about everything of interest in this process. If the study of language is limited in these ways, it seems inevitable that major aspects of verbal behavior will remain a mystery (p.58).

However, in spite of Chomsky's criticisms of the inadequacy of conditioning or reinforcement theories to explain language acquisition, such theories are still proposed. Staats and Staats (1962, 1963, 1968), for example, use such terms as *operant learning, reinforcing stimuli, time and scheduling of reinforcement, successive approximation, chaining, extinction,* and *discrimination and generalization* to explain how language is acquired. Such concepts can only weakly explain why all children exhibit much the same pattern of development, how they construct novel utterances even in the earliest days of language use, and in what ways they master the abstract relationships that are not readily apparent in the utterances they hear. This last point is extremely important because, as Garrett and Fodor (1968) argue, the facts of language are abstractions which children must acquire from masses of highly variable data. Language is a mentalistic phenomenon, and S-R theories are unable to account for either its acquisition or its use. The theory proposed by Staats and Staats involves the learning of a finite set of responses according to certain probabilities of occurrence. On the other hand, the current view is that a language is an infinite set of responses that are available to a speaker, and that language use is essentially creative. Probability has little to do with language use, although, of course, certain linguistic usages can be conditioned to events in the world *once such usages have been acquired.*

Jenkins and Palermo (1964) propose a theory of language acquisition that recognizes some recent linguistic advances. The basic problem they see in language acquisition is that of explaining how the child acquires the frames of a phrase-structure grammar and the ability to substitute items within these frames. They propose that the child learns the stimulus-and-response equivalences that can occur in the frames. They heavily emphasize imitation, either overt or covert, as a force in establishing bonds between stimuli and responses, and claim that the child generalizes to form classes of responses. However, they do not explain how control of such classes allows the child to construct longer sentences. Their theory does not attempt to analyze complex issues; it merely hints at them. The linguistic theory that Jenkins and Palermo propose is one N. Chomsky (1957) criticizes for being inadequate in that it does not account for the abstract nature of linguistic knowledge. Weksel (1965) is also critical of their proposal, claiming that it is linguistically inadequate and nowhere comes to grips with its central concept of generalization.

Another theory of language acquisition cast in the behavioristic mold comes from Braine (1963a, 1963b, 1965). This theory involves the principle of "contextual generalization," according to which the child observes that certain sets of items occur in certain positions. He makes generalizations about positions rather than about the sets of items that occupy them. The positions themselves are not simply linear, but may be hierarchical. Consequently, the theory attempts to explain how the child acquires the hierarchical grammatical structures of sentences. Braine claims that transformations can be learned through contextual generalization. If they cannot, he declares that the failure argues as much for a reshaping of linguistic theory as it does for a reshaping of the principle of contextual generalization.

> If there is a possibility that the simpler of two possible grammatical solutions might require the more complex acquisition theory, then the domain over which simplicity is taken cannot be restricted to grammar alone and must include acquisition theory—otherwise the grammarian merely purchases simplicity at the psychologist's expense (1965, p.491).

Slobin (1970a) objects to Braine's proposal, citing evidence from a variety of languages. Bever, Fodor, and Weksel (1965a, 1965b) argue that no dominant patterns of word order exist for the child to generalize from, even in a language such as English, and that word ordering also occurs during language acquisition even when the language has free word order. They say that the child must learn abstract structures for which no word-order patterns exist in the data to which he is exposed. Answering this last criticism, Braine (1965) points out that data do exist and that closer attention must be paid to how the child uses these data in the process of acquiring language.

NATIVIST THEORIES

Lenneberg (1967) proposes a theory of language acquisition heavily buttressed by biological evidence from studies of normal language development in children and of abnormal language development brought about congenitally, as in nanocephalic dwarfism, or environmentally, as in brain damage or aphasia. He emphasizes the development of the organism's capacities and shows how these mature along a fairly fixed schedule. Language emerges during this maturational process when anatomical, physiological, motor, neural, and cognitive developments allow it to emerge. Every child must learn the specific details of the language of his community, but the ability to learn language is innate and part of the biological endowment of the organism. The learning mechanisms, such as certain modes of perception, abilities in categorization, and capacities for transformation, are biologically given. According to Lenneberg, the child "resonates" to the language of his environment during the acquisition process; however, Lenneberg never clearly specifies exactly what resonance is. One of his most interesting observations is that there is a critical, biologically determined period for language acquisition between the ages of two and twelve.

Since Lenneberg is interested in the biological bases of language acquisition, he has almost nothing to say about how particular linguistic items are learned, except to deny that statistical probability and imitation are important in the process. He claims that language acquisition is a natural activity, much as learning to walk is a natural activity. Both activities occur universally unless a pathological condition exists. Learning, as this term is traditionally defined, is not involved. Instead, Lenneberg carefully locks language acquisition into the general biological development of the organism.

McNeill (1966, 1968, 1970a, 1970b) takes a rather different nativist position toward language acquisition. He says that anyone who wishes to study the problem of language acquisition must begin with a knowledge of what it is that the child must acquire:

> A major requirement for any theory of language acquisition is that it explain a known phenomenon, which means that theories of development must be related to particular grammatical analyses, to particular theories about language itself (1968, p.406).

McNeill claims that the child must acquire a generative-transformational grammar. Following N. Chomsky (1957, 1965), McNeill (1970a) asks what intrinsic properties must a device, a Language Acquisition Device (LAD), possess to acquire such a grammar from the corpus of utterances to which it is exposed:

> LAD is, of course, a fiction. The purpose in considering it is to discuss real children, not abstract ones. We can accomplish this because LAD and children present the same problem. LAD is faced with a corpus of utterances from which it develops a grammar on the basis of some kind of internal structure. So do children. We can readily posit that children and LAD arrive at the same grammar from the same corpus, and stipulate that children and LAD therefore have the same internal structure, at least within the limits that different children may be said to have the same internal structure. Accordingly, a theory about LAD is *ipso facto* a theory about children (p.71).

The child must possess certain innate abilities; otherwise it is impossible to explain how the random, finite, linguistic input into the child results in the output of linguistic competence.

According to McNeill, one innate property of the LAD is the ability to distinguish speech sounds from other sounds in the environment. A second property is the ability to organize linguistic events into various classes which can later be refined. This ability allows for the development of both the phonological and syntactic systems. One of the innate organizing principles is the concept of the "sentence." A third innate property is knowledge that only a certain lind of linguistic system is possible and that other kinds are not. McNeill claims that the child is born with an innate knowledge of linguistic universals. He distinguishes (1970a) between what he calls "weak" linguistic universals (reflections in language of universal cognitive abilities) and "strong" linguistic universals (reflections in language of specific linguistic abilities). He is more interested in the latter and seems skeptical of any claims advanced by cognitive theorists about the former. A fourth property is the ability to engage in constant evaluation of the developing linguistic system so as to construct the simplest possible system out of the linguistic data that are encountered.

In an attempt to justify his position, McNeill attacks S-R theory on the grounds that language acquisition is beyond its domain:

> Because S-R theory is so limited, the problem of language acquisition simply falls beyond its domain. This in itself is not a serious matter. Not all psychological theories need account for language acquisition. More serious, however, is the fact that the application of S-R principles causes theorists to redefine language in such a way as to make the phenomenon fit the theory. There is perhaps some irony in this outcome of modern empiricism (1968, p.412).

Using examples from Japanese, McNeill also argues against the importance of the frequency of stimuli in language acquisition, and against the importance of imitation. He claims that theories requiring imitation fail to explain why only certain responses occur. He criticizes Braine for ignoring the essential transformational nature of grammatical structure. Moreover, to Lenneberg's notion of a biological foundation for language, he adds a strong cognitive "content" component in the form of a structure for the mind that allows only certain kinds of language learning to occur. The organism has the capacity to learn and to generalize, but must realize this capacity within certain innate constraints that are suggested by a particular linguistic theory. McNeill actually says very little about the mechanisms of acquisition. In addition, his claim that in the earliest stages the child speaks in the universal base structures of a generative-transformational grammar may not be linguistically sound. His further claim that the child "honors" grammatical distinctions before actually making them has been attacked as invalid by Bloom (1971).

COGNITIVE THEORIES

Like Fodor (1968), Slobin (1966a, 1966b) does not subscribe to nativistic theories of language acquisition. He says:

> It seems to me that the child is born not with a set of linguistic categories but with some sort of process mechanism—a set of procedures and inference rules, if you will—that he uses to process linguistic data (1966b, pp.87-88).

Slobin regards language acquisition as an active process in which certain abilities of the child develop. One is the cognitive ability to deal with the world; a second is the mental ability to retain items in short-term memory, to store items in long-term memory, and to process information increasingly with age. The developments control the pace of language acquisition. Others are important too, such as the ability to segment utterances into sounds and meanings, and then to combine and recombine these segments, the ability to isolate meaning units, and the ability to make wide generalizations before attempting to accommodate exceptions. However, according to Slobin, general cognitive and mental development is the critical determinant of language acquisition.

Slobin marshals evidence from a variety of languages to support his position that language acquisition is one kind of general development, and that the general principles involved in the latter must be recognized. He differs from McNeill in the way he uses linguistic data. McNeill used such data to postulate the presence of innate linguistic principles; Slobin uses the same data to support innate principles of cognition. For example, in discussing McNeill's proposal concerning the child's innate knowledge of substantive linguistic universals, Slobin (1966b) says:

> Perhaps all that is needed is an ability to learn certain types of semantic or conceptual categories, the knowledge that learnable semantic criteria can be the basis for grammatical categories, and, along with this substantive

knowledge, the formal knowledge that such categories can be expressed by such morphological devices as affixing, sound alternation, and so on. The child's "preprogramming" for substantive universals is probably not for specific categories like past, animate, plural, and the like, but consists rather of the ability to learn categories of a certain as-yet-unspecified type (p.89).

Slobin differs from the behaviorist theorists in that he is a cognitive-learning theorist who regards the human learner as an active participant in learning rather than as a relatively passive reactor to external stimuli:

> The important advances in language development thus seem to be tied to such variables as increasing ability to perform a number of operations in a short time, increasing short-term memory span, and increasing cognition of the categories and processes of human experience. In fact, it may be that strictly *linguistic* acquisition is completed by age three or so. Further development may reflect lifting of performance restrictions and general cognitive growth, without adding anything basically new to the fundamental structures of syntactic competence. We have begun to gather data on the earliest stages of language development. We have very little data on later stages. And our understanding of the mental processes underlying the course of this development is extremely rudimentary indeed. At this point I believe we are in need of much more data on children's acquisition of various native languages...(1970b, p.184).

Cromer (1968) provides further evidence of the role of cognitive abilities in determining the language the child can use. From a study of the development of temporal reference in two children over a four-year period, he notes that several new types of reference to points in time begin to occur regularly at about the age of four to four and one-half for each child. Viewed together, these new forms indicate that the child has greatly expanded his range of temporal reference and increased his sense of the possible relations between times. Cromer notes that the child develops the ability to express events out of chronological order, to make statements about possibility, and to relate one time to another time. He hypothesizes that a single factor alone accounts for the observed linguistic changes: the child suddenly finds that he can free himself from the immediate situation and the actual order of events and can imagine himself at other points in time and view events from that perspective. This increase in his cognitive ability enables him to express new meanings, and he immediately masters the necessary syntactic apparatus to do so.

There are even stronger claims for a cognitive basis to language acquisition than those made by Slobin. Schlesinger (1971) claims that linguistic structures are "determined by the innate *cognitive* capacity of the child," and Sinclair-de-Zwart (1968) claims that "linguistic universals exist precisely because thought structures are universal." However, there is a scarcity of empirical evidence to support either claim.

LINGUISTICALLY-ORIENTED THEORIES VERSUS LEARNING-ORIENTED THEORIES

In trying to develop a theory of language acquisition, an investigator is faced with a fundamental decision concerning a starting point. Should he begin by accepting certain principles from linguistics or certain principles from psychology? In other words, should he begin by saying, as McNeill does, that what must be explained is how the child acquires a generative-transformational grammar, or by saying, as Staats and Staats do, that a behavioristic theory employing such principles as association formation and stimulus and response generalization should be able to account for language acquisition? McNeill proceeds to dismiss current learning theories as inadequate to explain the special behavior or knowledge which he claims comprises linguistic competence, and Staats and Staats proceed to ignore certain kinds of linguistic data.

Braine attempts to fasten on to the best in both linguistic theory and learning theory. He claims that each must, if necessary, be changed to accommodate the other. The two extremes of the general position taken by McNeill and by Staats and Staats are probably equally untenable, for at one extreme the interest is basically in the linguistic description of child language with very little concern for learning principles and at the other extreme the interest is in applying learning principles derived from experiments with animals to the one behavior that no animal .exhibits, linguistic behavior. Neither McNeill nor Staats and Staats take these extreme positions, but sometimes they seem to be approaching them. In the circumstances, Braine's middle ground may appear to be more attractive; however, both linguists and learning theorists find his proposed compromises unacceptable.

Fodor (1966) acknowledges the necessity for postulating some innate structure without committing himself as to whether this structure derives from innate linguistic principles or innate learning principles:

...the child must bring to the language learning situation some amount of intrinsic structure. This structure may take the form of general learning principles or it may take the form of relatively detailed and language-specific information about the kind of grammatical system that underlies natural languages. But what cannot be denied is that any organism that extrapolates from its experience does so on the basis of principles that are not themselves supplied by the experience (p. 106).

Slobin's position is less equivocal. He considers the child to be endowed with the cognitive capacity to perform extremely complicated tasks. The child accomplishes the complicated task of language acquisition according to general laws of development, learning, and perception. Consequently, he brings a particular capacity to the task rather than knowledge of a set of innate linguistic principles.

FOUR CONTROVERSIAL ISSUES

It is of interest to examine how various theories deal with the problems of the frequency of stimuli, the place of imitation, the role of expansion, and the function of meaning in language acquisition. In this way the theories can be shown to differ in certain important respects, and some preliminary assessment can be made of their relevance to beginning reading instruction.

The relative frequency of stimuli must be important in any behavioristic theory of learning. The most frequently occurring words and structures in the language should be acquired first by the child. However, the empirical evidence for language acquisition contradicts this expectation. Telegraphic speech, for example, omits the most frequently occurring words in the language and investigators agree that every child goes through a "telegraphic" stage. There must be some reason for the existence of such speech, but it appears to have little to do with the frequency of stimuli in the environment.

McNeill (1966, 1968) also argues that Japanese children acquire a less frequent grammatical marker *ga* before a more frequent marker *wa* because *ga* is important as a deep subject marker whereas *wa* is not. He later (1970a, pp.30-31) offers a rather different interpretation of the same data in accordance with the kinds of predicates (intrinsic with *wa* and extrinsic with *ga*) that the child is capable of forming at the age when *wa* and *ga* first appear in speech. Slobin (1970a) cites similar examples from other languages. If frequency is not important and certain kinds of learning occur in a definite progression, then the crucial issue is to account for this learning and the progression. McNeill argues that the structure of language and of the child's mind controls the learning, whereas Slobin argues that the child's cognitive and mental capacities at each stage regulate his ability to learn. However, each agrees with the other that the relative frequency of stimuli is of little importance in language acquisition.

Imitation in the sense of modeling also holds an important place in behavioristic theories of learning in which some kind of modeling of behavior must occur. While there is evidence that children do practice language (Weir, 1962) and do repeat some of the utterances of persons around them, they do not imitate indiscriminately. For example, Weir's child produced certain imitations but also made many variations on the imitated utterances. Babies do not imitate sounds in general, but they do respond quickly to human sounds. Lenneberg, Rebelsky, and Nichols (1965) also report that the prelinguistic vocalization behavior of deaf infants is no different from that of hearing infants. Therefore, imitation is not a critical factor in this very early stage of development, as it is, for example, in Jenkins and Palermo's (1964) theory. Menyuk (1963b) notes that the ability to imitate depends on the acquisition of some prior ability since children give evidence of various difficulties in imitating utterances. Utterances such as *allgone shoe, allgone lettuce,* and *allgone vitamins* reported by Braine (1963b) also argue against imitation and for some other ability for no such sentences occurred in the environment of the child who produced them. Similar evidence is reported by Brown and Bellugi (1964) and by Miller and Ervin (1964).

One obvious constraint upon the child's ability to imitate is the limitation imposed by his short-term memory span. It is also very difficult to explain how simple imitation leads to development. Obviously, some issue has been skirted. Young children are actually rather poor imitators, as McNeill (1966) demonstrates in the following sample:

> The signs are that sometimes a child's tendency to assimilate adult models into his current grammar is so strong that even when he makes a deliberate effort to copy adult speech, the effort may at first fail. One child, in the phase of producing double negatives while developing the negative transformation, had the following exchange with his mother:
> Child: Nobody don't like me

Mother: No, say "nobody likes me."
Child: Oh! Nobody don't likes me.
[eight repetitions of this dialogue]
Mother: No, now listen carefully; say *"nobody likes me."*
Child: Oh! Nobody don't likes me.
The exchange is interesting because it demonstrates the relative impenetrability of the child's grammar to adult models, even under the instruction (given by the mother's "no") to change. The child behaves at first as if he did not perceive the difference between his mother's sentence and his own, though later, when the mother supplied great emphasis, the child recognized a distinction. With this much delay in introducing changes, spontaneous imitations are bound not to be grammatically progressive because they consist only of a single exchange. The fact that a change ultimately was made, however, illustrates that children can profit from adult models (p.69).

McNeill does not deny the importance of models to the child in his learning, but does show that simple imitation of such models provides an inadequate explanation of linguistic development. Ervin (1964) demonstrates that imitations by children are not grammatically progressive, for they are less complicated syntactically than concurrent free utterances. Menyuk (1963a), Lenneberg, Nichols, and Rosenberger (1964), and Slobin and Welsh (1967) all report that children produce in imitation only what they produce in spontaneous speech even to the extent of reducing adult-given sentences to the forms they are currently producing.

Still another difficulty with relying heavily on imitation in any theory of language acquisition is the fact that much of the speech to which the child is exposed is considerably fragmented. Yet he learns to filter out poor examples in forming his grammar. This accomplishment is at least as difficult to explain as is the accomplishment of being able to react to more complex utterances than he can produce. Some factor other than imitation must be involved in each case. Lenneberg (1962) points out one specific case in which imitation could not have been involved in language acquisition, that of a boy with a congenital motor disability that prevented him from speaking. However, since the same boy could understand complicated instructions, neither imitation nor reinforcement could be used to explain his abilities. The language of the environment in which the child finds himself is vitally important to him in his acquisition of language. But direct imitation of that language seems not to occur except in rather small amounts.

The role of expansion in language acquisition is a still more complicated issue. Parents do correct and expand the speech of their children. However, there is evidence that children are not particularly receptive to direct instruction in language, as is obvious in the quotation cited above from McNeill. Although corrections might be expected to extinguish certain undesirable behaviors, they are unlikely to promote desirable ones. Expansions might be helpful in stimulating linguistic development, and some agreement exists that middle-class mothers expand their children's speech about 30% of the time and that such use of expansion forms a part of the normal mother-child relationship. Cazden (1965) tested the hypothesis that expansions of children's utterances would aid language acquisition more than would comments on their utterances, which she called models, and that both would produce better results than no expansion or modeling responses. She divided twelve 2½-year-old children into three groups: the first group received intensive and deliberate expansions; the second group received qualitatively equal exposure to well-formed sentences that were models, not expansions; and the third group received no special treatment at all. Her experiment lasted twelve weeks. The results do not show quite the expected differences; modeling, not expansion, was more effective. That is, semantically enriched responses were more effective than syntactically enriched responses. However, a more recent study by Feldman and Rodgon (1970) reports results at variance with those of Cazden. In a further study, Brown, Cazden, and Bellugi (1968) analyzed the conversations of mothers and children aged one to four years to determine what happens during such conversations. They report that the syntactic correctness or incorrectness of a child's speech does not control the mother's approval or disapproval. Rather the truth or falsity of the utterance does. They conclude that parents tend to reward true statements and punish false ones; however, the result is the eventual production of syntactically correct sentences.

Deliberate expansion of children's language by adults would seem to be one of the most important possible influences on language development. However, the evidence does not confirm this hypothesis. Having considered the evidence from research in the use of both imitation and expansion, Slobin (1968) concludes that there is little evidence to support imitation. However, he takes a more positive attitude toward expansion:

> It has been suggested that frequency of parental expansion of child speech may be related to such variables as social class and education, and, in turn, be

partly responsible for differences in language acquisition and ability in children of different socioeconomic backgrounds. The issue is certainly complex, and we are far from being able to determine the function—if any—of expansion and imitation in the human child's remarkable acquisition of language. Until the necessary data are amassed, I would still like to believe that when a child hears an adult expansion of his own speech he learns something important about the structure of his language (p.443).

The results as a whole argue more for the acceptance of language-acquisition theories like those of Lenneberg,. McNeill, and Slobin than they do for those of Braine and Staats and Staats, and more for the importance of some kind of innate linguistic or cognitive structure than of the actual stimuli encountered in the environment.

Studies of language acquisition tend to focus on the acquisition of phonology or syntax. The place and function of meaning in language acquisition have largely been ignored. However, meaning is today assuming greater importance in studies of language acquisition.

Following a comprehensive review of Russian data on language development in children, Slobin (1966a) suggests that the order of emergence of various syntactic categories depends on their relative semantic difficulty rather than on their grammatical complexity. The first grammatical distinctions to appear are those like the singular-plural distinction that make some concrete reference to the outside world. Later to emerge are the diminutive suffixes of nouns, imperatives, and categories based on relational criteria, such as the case, tense, and person markings of verbs. Conditional forms of the *if-then* variety are not learned until near the end of the third year. Still other abstract categories of quality and action continue to be added until the age of seven. Slobin argues that semantic complexity rather than grammatical difficulty determines the developmental sequence. Grammatical gender in Russian is the most difficult of all the categories for the child to master since it has almost no semantic correlates. No rules exist that the child can discover to make the learning easier, so the acquisition of gender is a long, drawn-out process. Slobin (1966a) concludes: "The semantic and conceptual aspects of grammatical classes thus clearly play an important role in determining the order of their development and subdivision" (p.142).

Telegraphic speech is full of "contentive" words. Slobin (1971, pp.44-46) shows some of the semantic range of telegraphic speech in various languages: English, German, Russian, Finnish, Luo, and Samoan. Following an analysis of such speech, a reexamination of the data from the pivot grammars of investigators such as Braine, and some work of her own, Bloom (1970) argues that the evidence indicates that semantic competence outstrips syntactic competence. Her own research showed that noun-noun combinations in the speech of very young English children expressed at least the following five relations: conjunction (*block dolly*), attribution (*party hat*), genitive (*daddy hat*), subject-locative (*sweater chair*), and subject-object (*mommy book*). She also found that an utterance such as *no truck* could have various meanings, which themselves showed an order of emergence: "nonexistence" (*There's no truck here*) preceding "rejection" (*I don't want a truck*), which in turn precedes "denial" (*It's not a truck; it's something else*). She concludes that the child's underlying semantic competence is more differentiated than the surface forms of his utterances, because he is aware of more types of meaning relationships than he can reveal through the linguistic devices he controls. Before he develops these devices, his two-word utterances can only be properly interpreted through the use of the nonlinguistic context. Quite often a young child must produce a series of short utterances in order to convey information that an adult or an older child expresses in a single utterance. For example, he might say *raisin there / buy more grocery store / raisins / buy more grocery store / grocery store / raisin a grocery store* instead of one sentence about buying more raisins at the grocery store. Consequently, Bloom (1970) claims that three components operate in the development of language competence: cognitive-perceptual development; linguistic experience; and nonlinguistic experience. She notes that these components converge during the child's development.

AN ASSESSMENT OF THE THEORIES

The studies reported by McCarthy encompass massive quantities of data but lack clearly defined theories of language acquisition. A concern for such theories is a fairly recent development in studies of language acquisition. However, all such theories have at least the weaknesses of lack of detail and lack of empirical validation. They are all very general, often being little more than series of claims about what must be, the claims being supported by reference to carefully selected data often acquired from no more than a few children. Consequently, they are often hardly any more convincing than former presentations of large quantities of data that really make no claims at all.

Recently proposed theories make either a language or learning component central. Making a language component central requires postulation of a strong innate predisposition toward the acquisition of very specific kinds of linguistic facts, for the child is assumed to *know* much about language in general before any learning of specific details begins. Environmental factors are relatively unimportant in such theories. On the other hand, older behavioristic learning theories hold the environment to be extremely important in providing language stimuli and controlling the learning that occurs. According to such theories, language acquisition is achieved through such processes as association and response generalization. The child makes little or no active contribution to the total process and learns language in much the same way as he learns anything else.

A less extreme position is that language acquisition is unique because language is different from anything else that is learned, but that the learning requires use of many of the same principles as other kinds of learning. In this case, the theory may have a large biological component that emphasizes the importance of certain kinds of meaningful situations that stimulate language acquisition and the cognitive limitations that human development places on the acquisition process. Unfortunately, since meaning has long been a stepchild in linguistics and cognitive theory a poor relation in psychology, it is difficult at present to fill out the details of any such theory.

An evaluation of the importance of such factors as frequency, imitation, and expansion in language acquisition leads to the rejection of any kind of monolithic behavioristic theory. However, it does not eliminate linguistically-based theories nor does it contradict cognitively-based ones. The evaluation reveals how unimportant each of the factors is in language acquisition, and indicates the necessity of crediting the child with some kind of innate knowledge of capacity. The difficulty with the innate-knowledge hypothesis is that investigators like McNeill have very little to say about the mechanisms through which that knowledge reveals itself, nor do they try to relate language learning to other kinds of learning. The result is something less than a parsimonious view of total human development. The advantage of the innate-capacity hypothesis is that general laws of learning, but not exclusively behavioristic ones, can be used to explain both language acquisition and other kinds of learning. Sachs (1971) summarizes this problem as follows:

Theories of language acquisition that consider only the linguistic aspect will not be able to explain why the child learns new forms when he does, or in fact why he ever changes his form of expression. It is only through more research on the complex relationship between cognitive development and language acquisition that we will have a full understanding of either. Hopefully in the future we will find more studies of this type, and a closer communication between psycholinguists and psychologists studying other aspects of child development (p.394).

The linguistically based theories all have one serious drawback in that they are concerned with the ideal child. Theories recognizing individual and group differences are ignored in favor of theories that try to account for the development of abstract linguistic competence. Social, motivational, and cultural variables are all ignored. The child is said to have acquired his basic linguistic competence by the age of five or six. While performance is acknowledged to vary from child to child, such variability, whatever its cause, is ignored, often under the guise of "performance" differences, which are at best of peripheral interest. The result is a deliberate biasing of the theories toward accommodating one set of factors in language acquisition and ignoring almost all others.

LANGUAGE ACQUISITION AFTER AGE SIX

Although many linguists claim that the major part of language acquisition takes place in the years between the ages of one and four, children who enter school do not have the linguistic abilities of adults. Furthermore, the linguistic abilities of adults change, and sometimes develop, during their lives. It is of interest to know the precise differences between the linguistic abilities of children entering school and of adults. Numerous investigators have shown that significant language development still occurs in all children after the age of five or six, among them Harrell (1957), Strickland (1962), Loban (1963), Menyuk (1963b), and O'Donnell, Griffin, and Norris (1967).

In a recent study, C. S. Chomsky (1969) points out several grammatical developments that occur during the years that follow six: a grasp of the differences between the *eager to see* and *easy to see* constructions; a realization that *ask* and *tell* require different syntactic constructions; the ability to handle relationship requiring *and* and *although*; and a control of pronominalizations. Kessel (1970) used a Piaget-type interview technique similar to that used by C. S. Chomsky in further work on some of the same problems. His study confirms her results but also reports evidence of a somewhat earlier mastery of the more complex constructions. Menyuk (1969) points out other examples in which a more complicated structure is learned later than a less complicated one. However, in every case it is possible to argue that the linguistic development has not occurred because the cognitive capacities of the child did not allow it rather than because the structure which is learned second is more complicated than the one which is learned first. Of course, since it is also possible to argue that the structure learned second is grammatically more complicated, the temptation is to postulate a linguistic rather than a cognitive constraint on development, particularly when the investigator is linguistically-oriented.

Two linguistic abilities that children of about age six appear to have are those to overdiscriminate and to overgeneralize. N. Chomsky (1964) points out that they have very sharp abilities to discriminate among phonetically close stimuli. Ervin (1964) and Miller and Ervin (1964) say that they tend to eliminate from their language irregular but correct inflections in favor of regular but incorrect ones for a while. Slobin (1970a), citing evidence mainly from Russian, discusses this same phonomenon, which he calls "inflectional imperialism." Bever, Mehler, and Valian (1968) report that children aged two to four temporarily overgeneralize newly acquired semantic strategies. There is also some agreement that children do not interpret "same" and "different" in the way that mature adults do, nor are they able to work in a conscious analytic fashion with language, as many adults can. Slobin (1970a) points out that the Russian data he analyzed provide evidence that any kind of direct instruction in the analysis of language is rather ineffective with children.

In one crucial area for any kind of reading instruction that relies on the relationship of individual sounds to symbols, the acquisition of phonology, six-year-olds have not mastered the system that educated literate adults appear to have mastered (Chomsky and Halle, 1968; C. S. Chomsky, 1970). The abilities of the two groups appear to be quite different. *Indeed language acquisition in this area appears to depend on the acquisition of the ability to read, but this is the only place where this particular dependency occurs.*

SOME IMPORTANT DIFFERENCES BETWEEN LANGUAGE ACQUISITION AND BEGINNING READING

Whatever theory of language acquisition an investigator subscribes to, behavioristic, nativistic, or cognitive, he must readily admit that important differences exist between the acquisition of language and the acquisition of beginning reading skills. Staats and Staats (1962), Carrol (l966c), and Natchez (1967) are among those who point out some of the specific differences.

Language is acquired gradually and the acquisition process is probably never completed, for something always remains to be learned. The process is also one that had no conscious beginning point for the child. On the other hand, learning to read often has a sudden onset for children, although some are fortunate to avoid this kind of introduction. Even though some of the cognitive and motor skills necessary for reading have been developed for other activities, the child is often required to put them all together rather abruptly in learning to read in a formal school setting.

The level of anxiety in the context in which learning to read takes place may also be quite high: the anxiety of the parent, teacher, and the child. Little such anxiety is manifested during the process of learning to talk. Certainly, it is the rare child who exhibits anxiety, and, if the occasional parent is anxious about a particular child's speech, this anxiety seems to have little influence on the child's language development. There is also often a concomitant assignment of blame for any failure that occurs in beginning reading instruction. Children are not blamed when they fail to acquire language; rather, they are given special help.

Reading instruction is very formal and deliberate. Language, however, is learned informally and unconsciously from a wide range of stimuli. No deliberate instruction is necessary. Language is not learned from programed stimuli, from making conscious distinctions among stimuli, from learning *about* language, and from acquiring control of a variety of analytic and synthetic techniques. While controversy does exist as to the function of linguistic stimuli in language acquisition, there is agreement that such stimuli vary in both form and content in ways that are not well understood, but which the child is well able to handle.

The usual reinforcements experienced by literate adults for reading may be irrelevant for many children in the beginning reading stages; the benefits are often too abstract, distant, and meaningless, and the effort to be expended for such remote ends may seem to be quite wasteful and unpleasant to the child. On the other hand, the benefits of learning to speak are too obvious to mention.

The two activities are also different in certain other ways. Learning to read depends on the acquisition of special skills in visual discrimination. The redundancies in the two language systems that are involved are also different, as is quite often the content, that is the meanings that are conveyed. Writing is not simply speech written down: it is more abstract than speech in content; it usually employs carefully edited and controlled language for reasons different from speaking; and it functions rather differently in the lives of the recipients of the message. Vygotsky (1962) writes as follows on these very points, but in connection with writing rather than reading:

> Written speech is a separate linguistic function, differing from oral speech in both structure and mode of functioning. Even its minimal development requires a high level of abstraction....Our studies show that it is the abstract quality of written language that is the main stumbling block, not the underdevelopment of small muscles or any other mechanical obstacles.

> Writing is also speech without an interlocutor, addressed to an absent or an imaginary person or to no one in particular—a situation new and strange to the child. Our studies show that he has little motivation to learn writing when we begin to teach it. He feels no need for it and has only a vague idea of its usefulness. In conversation, every sentence is prompted by a motive. Desire or need lead to request, question to answer, bewilderment to explanation. The changing motives of the interlocutors determine at every moment the turn oral speech will take. It does not have to be consciously directed—the dynamic situation takes care of that. The motives for writing are more abstract, more intellectualized, further removed from immediate needs. In written speech, we are obliged to create the situation, to represent it to ourselves. This demands detachment from the actual situation.

> Writing also requires deliberate analytical action on the part of the child. In speaking, he is hardly conscious of the sounds he pronounces and quite unconscious of the mental operations he performs. In writing, he must take cognizance of the sound structure of each word, dissect it, and reproduce it in alphabetical symbols which he must have studied and memorized before (pp. 98-99).

Reid (1966), Meltzer and Herse (1969), and Downing (1970) all point to the confusion that children often experience in learning to read. Evidently, many children do not understand what reading is, or what they are supposed to be doing, or what the terms mean that are used in the instructional process.

The usual methods of reading instruction employ imitation, repetition, control of stimuli, correction, and expansion—exactly those factors examined earlier in relation to the acquisition of language. These factors were found not to be very important in language acquisition; however, they are very important in reading instruction. Of course, instruction implies some kind of methodology, so the reason for their existence is obvious. Yet, it would be well to subject that methodology to periodic critical assessment in the light of the latest findings from relevant disciplines. Of course, one can also argue that since language acquisition and learning to read are quite different tasks, these factors may still be important in the teaching of beginning reading.

Finally, language acquisition does not cease at age six. Consequently, some kinds of acquisition overlap with learning to read. However, little is known about the extent of this overlap, for the later stages of language acquisition are just as much a mystery as are the earlier stages. It may be that more than one of these stages depends on the child's acquiring certain reading abilities just as beginning reading ability quite definitely depends on the acquisition of considerable linguistic competence. However, this acquisition has occurred in six-year-olds except in rare pathological cases.

CONCLUSION

The theories of language acquisition that are available to us today are largely irrelevant in deciding issues in beginning-reading instruction or even in devising models of the reading process. Moreover, reading failure cannot easily be linked to deficiencies in language acquisition for children who are asked to learn to read are almost invariably well on the way to linguistic maturity.

Reading methods themselves are almost unrelated to the theories of language acquisition. Both phonics and whole-word methods depend on the possession of certain language abilities which all children of six apparently possess. What they might not have are some of the cognitive abilities that the methods require: abilities to make certain kinds of discriminations, to form generalizations, and to verbalize knowledge. Furthermore, much of what is taught *about* language in such methods is antiquated and not very useful to anyone, particularly to six-year-olds.

Reading is often taught to improve language. Research has long demonstrated that such teaching is generally ineffective. Some linguistic skills apparently derive from the acquisition of the skills of literacy, but these skills appear to be few and certainly do not seem to be acquired during the critical period of beginning reading instruction.

chapter nine
A New Perspective on Reading

When a person reads a text, he must discover the meaning of what he is reading by using familiar spelling clues, a knowledge of probabilities of occurrence of words and expressions, his grammatical competence, and both contextual and pragmatic knowledge in order to interpret the text meaningfully. Reading is not simply a passive process which requires the reader only to take things out of the text by performing various simple recognition tasks. Reading does not appear to be a process which requires the reader first to recognize something on the page and then to interpret what he recognizes. There is no reason to suppose the existence of two such discrete, non-overlapping stages. Reading is a process which requires the reader to make an active contribution by drawing upon and using concurrently various abilities that he has acquired.

READING AS ACTIVE INFORMATION-PROCESSING

The abilities a reader must use are of many different kinds. One is the ability to associate certain sounds and certain letters. The reader must be able to react to significant rather than nonsignificant visual clues if he is to achieve good speed and flexibility in his reading. He must also be able to use both his short-term and his long-term memories effectively during the processing required in reading, for he cannot afford to forget significant information. Such abilities are not used automatically in all circumstances because even the best readers make mistakes which indicate that the required processing was either incompletely or inaccurately carried out. Moreover, the processing itself is not just processing of visual signals in order to convert these signals into some kind of covert speech. It is not simply a conversion of spellings to sounds no matter how internalized those sounds are said to be. Any conversion that does take place is not the end point of the process since additional semantic and syntactic processing is necessary.

Semantic and syntactic processing requires the reader to know the language, that is to be linguistically competent, and to use this knowledge actively. No one can read a foreign language, except perhaps to pronounce it, unless he has some degree of underlying competence in that language together with training in its orthographic principles and a familiarity with the subject matter. Likewise, a child cannot learn to read English unless he has some underlying competence in English, some awareness of the conventions of English orthography, and some assurance that the actual content of the material he is asked to read relates to matters within his experience. In such circumstances he is likely to find the task of learning to read to be a meaningful one, and he is likely to be successful in that task.

In teaching beginning-reading skills we cannot avoid placing emphasis on the relationship between spelling and pronunciation. As has been indicated on several occasions, this relationship is not as simple as certain claims have made it out to be. Furthermore, certain claims about the relationships of symbols to sounds are open to question, for example, claims about the function of "silent" or "internalized" speech. Likewise, statements about what is regular and irregular in English spelling and how and why the irregularities must be controlled in beginning-reading texts are sometimes conflicting, because no universal agreement exists on exactly how English spelling represents English pronunciation. Conflicting opinions exist, too, about the usefulness of modified English spelling systems. In the area of syntax there is discussion about the desirability of restricting the content of readers to some of the simple recurring superficial patterns of the child's spoken language and excluding patterns that are either infrequent or complex.

Linguists cannot provide final answers to many of these problems because the problems are not exclusively linguistic in nature: other variables than linguistic ones must be considered. Such problems are mainly pedagogical, so while linguists can provide some help in finding solutions, they cannot provide total solutions. There is, therefore, no more justification for talking about a linguistic method of teaching reading than for talking about a linguistic method of teaching foreign languages. Linguistic methods are methods for doing linguistic research, and the teaching of reading is not part of linguistic research. Reading instruction should have a large linguistic content, but it must also have content that is nonlinguistic; consequently, methods for teaching reading must draw on other sources in addition to linguistic ones. However, such methods should build on sound linguistic knowledge if they are not to fly in the face of common sense.

We can observe too that children will learn to read only by being given help with just that task: they do not learn to read by being told *about* reading. They do not learn to read by learning rules about what to do when they are confronted with certain difficulties, particularly when these rules are either too sophisticated, complicated, or inconsistent to be applied with a reasonable chance of success. Instead, children must learn to relate certain sounds to certain symbols, to distinguish *d* from *b* and *mat* from *mate*, to recognize that left-to-right direction is important, as in *dog* and *god* and *top desk* and *desk top*, to recognize that the syntax of the written language is basically the same as that of the spoken language, and to use contextual clues in resolving problems and ambiguities. A few very basic rules such as those that apply to the *c* in *city* and *cat*, the *igh* in *fight*, and the *x* in *box* may be useful to beginning readers; however, teaching children long lists of unordered phonic generalizations is likely to harm them rather than help them in their learning task.

Children obviously learn sets of rules of one kind or another for use in reading, because they do learn to read with greater or lesser success. Even their mistakes are often instances of the choice of inappropriate rules rather than randomized behaviors. A child learns to read *city* and *cat* correctly as the result of experience with words beginning with *ci-* and *ca-*. He unconsciously assimilates the rule that *c* followed by one group of vowel letters almost always represents an [s] sound and *c* followed by another group of vowel letters almost always represents a [k] sound. The child may not be able to verbalize the rule, any more than he can tell how it is that he is able to walk on two legs, but just as he can demonstrate that he knows the "rules" for walking by walking, so he can demonstrate his knowledge of the rules for pronouncing *c* by reading *city* and *cat* correctly. He demonstrates his knowledge of the rules in his performance, and it is quite unnecessary for him to learn to verbalize statements about what he has learned, that is about what he knows, his competence. In studying the linguistic and reading performance of children, a teacher should attempt to understand the unconscious rules a particular child is applying to the tasks which confront him. The teacher would also be wise to see the child's total behavior as rule-governed, and regard "mistakes" as instances of the application of inappropriate rules rather than as the results of random behavior.

The whole concept of "mistake" and "error" could well be discarded in favor of such an approach. Admittedly, not every mistake will be explicable in these terms, but it seems more fruitful to hypothesize that "mistakes result from the application of rules which are different from the rules of mature language users" than to hypothesize that "mistakes are instances of random(or perverse) behavior."

Reading requires certain perceptual skills not required in speaking and, conversely, does not require certain perceptual skills required in speaking. The claim has been made that when we read we "hear" what we read, the visual symbol somehow triggering an aural one. While some evidence exists for silent speech (Edfeldt, 1960) and for the claim that speech perception has a motor basis, this evidence is by no means conclusive since contradictory evidence can also be cited: receptive control of language always exceeds productive control; silent reading speed often exceeds aural comprehension speed; and some people learn to read English who cannot or do not speak English for various reasons. While every normal human being has the capacity for language acquisition, this capacity can apparently be realized by linguistic stimuli other than aural stimuli, even though the latter are those to which most people actually do respond. A normal child reacts naturally to the spoken language that surrounds him. It provides him with all the stimuli he needs to become a speaker of the language and realize his innate language-learning potential. A child who is not normal, who is deaf or dumb or both, still has this potential but must react to different external stimuli. His task may be much more difficult, but it is probably never impossible.

Reading itself is a different kind of linguistic performance from listening, just as listening is from speaking. The possible range of understanding in listening is greater than the range of production in speaking, and the range of understanding of written material is usually greater than that of spoken material. We can read and reread, and thereby control the speed of the processing of the content that we are reading. The content of what is read is often rather different from the content of listening, however, and such differences can create difficulties. In general, written language is more deliberate, more complex, more heavily edited, and less redundant than spoken language. It also offers no opportunity to question the writer in order to seek clarification of his statements unlike many of the situations in which spoken language is used.

In both kinds of performance the individual makes a large personal contribution to understanding the language stimuli that are coming to him. As often as not he hears what he wants to hear and reads what he wants to read rather than hears or reads what was actually said or written. Comprehension is an active process not a passive one. The comprehender must continually make hypotheses about what he is hearing or reading, attempt to match these hypotheses with other data that are available to him, and modify the hypotheses if they prove to be inadequate.

On occasions people adopt processing strategies that result in selective listening or reading. These strategies allow them to ignore data that do not conform to their hypotheses and result in a mishearing or misreading of the original content, a type of "mistake" that is a direct consequence of the contribution of the comprehender to the process of comprehension. For example, we sometimes anticipate words in a conversation or text only to discover ourselves to be wrong, or we do not wait for sentences to be completed because we assume we know what their endings will be, or we miss spelling mistakes because we are more concerned with meaning than with proofreading. Many of the mistakes students make in reading are made because they have adopted inappropriate strategies for the particular task that was required. In the later stages of reading instruction, when reading for implications and reading between the lines become important, the possibilities for the use of inappropriate strategies increase. That errors and mistakes do occur in these circumstances is to be expected; perhaps it would even be wise to avoid using such terms as *error* and *mistake* in discussing these kinds of linguistic performance. The errors and mistakes are often perfectly explicable, because of their rule-governed nature.

READING COMPETENCE AND READING PERFORMANCE

Goodman (1967) has made one of the most interesting attempts to explain what happens when children make mistakes in reading. He has shown that in reading unfamiliar textual material, children are forced to play a "psycholinguistic guessing game." A child reading an unfamiliar or difficult text must draw upon the reading rules he has internalized. He must try out his knowledge of sound-symbol relationships, grammatical patterning, semantic groupings, and the real world in his attempt to impose some kind of meaning on the text. He must draw on different varieties of knowledge concurrently, and he must make hypotheses, that is educated guesses. Sometimes his guesses will be incorrect and his responses will not conform to those of a mature reader. However, his guesses will rarely be completely random: they will be "miscues" in Goodman's terms rather than mistakes. Such miscues can provide a reading researcher with a great deal of insight into the particular strategies that the child is using, that is the psycholinguistic processes he is employing subconsciously. A reader's miscues in reading provide evidence that his competence in reading varies from that of an ideal reader, not that he lacks reading competence.

Reading competence is different from linguistic competence, but the two are not completely unrelated. Both uses of the term refer to ideal systems: the linguist's term refers to the ideal system that he uses to characterize language ability: the reading researcher's term refers to the system that the reader has access to in his attempts to comprehend what he is reading. This system must include the linguistic competence of the reader that is relevant to his task. But it also must include non-linguistic factors, because reading is both a perceptual and a cognitive task and involves many competences beyond the one which interests the linguist. Both kinds of competence must be distinguished from related performances, for both speakers and readers make mistakes, find their memories overburdened, and get confused as they react to inappropriate stimuli. However, such phenomena must be clearly distinguished from those that directly appear to manifest competence. People generally know when they have made a mistake, when they cannot remember how a sentence began, and when they are confused. And readers quite often recognize that they are not reading as well as they should be reading because they are making mistakes which they normally do not make.

LANGUAGE AND READING

The teaching of reading must be clearly distinguished from the teaching of speaking. Children come to school already speaking a dialect of the language, and it should be possible to teach them to read by drawing upon the language competence they exhibit in that dialect. An important distinction should be made between students who have certain kinds of performance limitations, such as memory, perceptual, and motor limitations, and students who speak nonstandard dialects. The former students have congenital or acquired deficiencies for which reading teachers must compensate. The latter students may or may not exhibit some of the same problems and as a group may actually have a greater incidence of such problems because of various factors in their background, but they should not be treated in the same way as the first group when they do not have such problems.

A student who says *Ruf* because he has a physical defect should be treated quite differently from one who says *Ruf* because that pronunciation of *Ruth* is a feature of his dialect. To send both students to the speech therapist for identical "treatments" is a serious mistake. The same may be true of pronunciations like *wed* for *red*, *Buce* for *Bruce*, and *fevver* for *feather*. Such pronunciations should not be regarded as creating obstacles in learning to read. A teacher might be tempted to accept the pathological or maturational *Ruf* and condemn the dialectal *Ruf* but such a reaction would show a misunderstanding of language function. Poor articulation and poor enunciation have little to do with reading success and failure or with anything that might be called normal language use. A pronunciation such as *Ruf* is at most a symptom of either a minor pathological defect or a dialect difference; in either case it is the cause that should be treated, not the symptom. However such treatment is worthwhile only if the particular pathological cause can be remedied or if it is considered desirable to make a standard dialect available to the speaker.

READING AND DISCOVERY

Reading instruction should take place within a total language program of which it forms an important part. The total program should allow students the chance to make discoveries about how language is used. It should try to avoid prescribing how language should be used, as most programs do at present. There are at least two reasons for this needed change in emphasis. The first is that the discovery approach conforms better to good linguistic, psychological, and pedagogical principles than does a prescriptive approach. The second is that understanding a process is likely to lead to better use of that process, but only if that understanding results from meaningful rather than rote learning. Because of its diversity of forms and uses language is a fascinating subject for study, which can provide a wealth of meaningful exploratory experiences for students of all ages. Children are naturally inquisitive and they may be encouraged to explore their linguistic environment in the same way that they are encouraged to explore the surrounding fields, woods, streets, and stores. This exploration is likely to be very useful to children as they begin to understand the linguistic environment, discover its possibilities, and use these findings to further their interests.

The actual finding-out process can make use of various types of experiences and strategies within an overall pattern of teaching that is eclectic rather than stereotyped. Children are different, teachers are different, and language has a multitude of different facets. No one royal road to learning exists; rather there are a great many paths, few of which are very straight. Children should be exposed to a variety of linguistic experiences according to their needs and abilities. Language is uniform and consistent only in the abstract forms described by linguists; in real life it is extremely diverse, just as the people who use it are very diverse. Students cannot learn to savor this diversity if the curriculum offers every student exactly the same linguistic diet. It is in such a context that reading instruction should be placed. The results should be better than those achieved at present because of the extra dimensions that will be brought to this instruction from the area of language study and from a pedagogy which recognizes and fosters individual differences and individual development.

part four

Linguistics
and
Second-Language Teaching

chapter ten

Teaching English to Speakers of Other Languages

In the last twenty years the teaching of English to speakers of other languages within the United States has become an increasingly important concern within the educational system. The clientele is vast, including foreign students on university and college campuses, foreign nationals taking specialized types of training in military or industrial establishments, large groups of immigrants in certain regions (for example, in and around Miami), and native-born non-English-speaking United States citizens (for example, citizens of Spanish and American-Indian ancestry). Nearly all ages, language backgrounds, cultures, and standards of educational attainment are represented in this clientele. In recent years too there has been an attempt to add to it those speakers of varieties of nonstandard English who, it is claimed, should learn Standard English as if it were an entirely new language.

All of this activity is in addition to the effort expended in teaching English in non-English-speaking countries. In this latter kind of activity many types of organizations find involvement. Some, like UNESCO, are international in scope, while others are national governmental agencies, as for example the United States Information Agency, the Agency for International Development, the Department of State, the Peace Corps (or Action), and so on of the United States, and the British Council of the United Kingdom. Private foundations have also provided support to overseas programs either in the form of "seed" money or for short-term projects. And, of course, within such countries the English departments of schools, colleges, and universities and interested groups within business, industry, and the professions have played a considerable part in the development of training programs in English.

LINGUISTICS AND LANGUAGE TEACHING

A reading of the recent history of teaching English to speakers of other languages and of many of the recent books and articles on specific pedagogical issues reveals that the present state of the art must be characterized by the word *uncertainty*. This uncertainty arises from the current ferment in those disciplines which underlie second language teaching: linguistics, psychology, and pedagogy. It is also reflected in teacher training and in the materials being produced for classroom use.

Until as recently as a decade ago it appeared that a major breakthrough had occurred in teaching foreign languages. In vogue was a method variously described as the *Aural-Oral, Audiolingual,* or even *Linguistic Method,* a method that derived much of its novelty from the discipline of linguistics. It appeared to many linguists that language was speech, that speech preceded writing in various ways, that the contrastive systems of phonology and grammar could be described with considerable accuracy, and that knowledge of a language as a system for conveying meanings was somehow more important than knowledge of the meanings themselves. Allied to certain ideas in learning theory, such as habit formation and interference, and to notions of programing or sequencing of materials, this linguistic knowledge seemed to promise a new era in language teaching. In such teaching, emphasis was to be placed on teaching the spoken language, on teaching a language as a system, on establishing this system as a set of habits, and on reducing the learning burden by teaching only those features of the second language that contrasted with features in the first language.

In 1957, however, the publication of *Syntactic Structures* by Noam Chomsky revolutionized linguistics. Chomsky called into question the basic tenets of the discipline of linguistics, outlined a set of new assumptions, and formulated a set of entirely new questions for the discipline to address itself to. It is impossible to understand current issues in teaching English to speakers of other languages without having some understanding of the linguistic theory associated with Chomsky.

Generative-transformational theory stresses the creative, rule-governed nature of the linguistic knowledge of a native speaker and attempts to set up criteria by which various models of this knowledge may be evaluated. These models have been called *competence* models in that they are concerned with ideal linguistic behavior in an ideal setting. They are not concerned with performance, that is actual linguistic behavior, nor are they concerned with psychological processes. Linguistic competence is said to underlie linguistic performance and to explain part of that performance: grammars themselves are *not* to be taken as performance models. Chomsky further discusses these notions of competence and performance in *Language and Mind* (1968).

The models express a different relationship of sounds to meanings from the models used by structural linguists. No longer are phonological, grammatical, and semantic systems discussed as though they were independent of each other. Instead, either syntax or semantics is made central and the other two components (semantics and phonology, or syntax and phonology) are made subordinate. Linguists use these models in an attempt to explain how a speaker decides the content of what he wants to say and produces that content in some kind of substance. The description of the content is sometimes called the *deep structure* and that of the substance the *surface structure*; however, no precise definition exists of what either of these terms means, how the levels which they denote may be distinguished if they exist, and how deep structures become surface structures through transformational processes.

Some of the difficulties that arise in teaching English to speakers of other languages may be illustrated by reference to certain specific problems in syntax, phonology, and meaning. We must note that the various linguistic insights that emerge do not determine any particular teaching method or methods. Too often in the past it has been assumed that a linguistic technique could be made into a pedagogical technique (for example, the "minimal pair" technique) or that insights into linguistic structure achieved by linguists should be communicated rather directly to learners. In the discussion that follows linguistic insights are separated from pedagogical concerns of one kind or another.

Generative-transformational linguists have stressed the importance of relationships between sets of sentences such as those represented in the pairs 1-2, 3-4, 5-6, 7-8, and 9-10:

1 The boy chased the dog.
2 The dog was chased by the boy.

3 The boy came. The boy is little.
4 The little boy came.

5 I asked Tom something. Tom wanted something.
6 I asked Tom what he wanted.

7 Someone opened the door.
8 The door was opened.

9 You will eat your dinner.
10 Eat your dinner!

In each case there is a good theoretical reason to claim a "primacy" for the odd-numbered member(s) of each pair over the even-numbered member, because the former may be said to underlie the latter in some way, though the ways are different in each case. Likewise, 11 may be said to be more basic than 12, even though 12 is more likely to be heard than 11:

11 Where are you going? I am going to the library.
12 Where are you going? To the library.

Generative-transformationalists have also stressed the importance of ambiguous utterances such as 13 and 14:

13 They have discarded clothes.
14 Girl Hunter Says Father Sets Example

They insist that an adequate grammar must have devices for resolving the ambiguity of such utterances, so that 13 can be interpreted as a statement about either social **workers or nudists** and 14 as a newspaper headline about either the daughter of a hunter or the playboy son of a playboy father. They also point out that sentences 15-17 are identical in certain aspects of surface arrangement but basically are rather different, as can be shown by both the possible and impossible paraphrases indicated in 18-20:

15 The boy is easy to please.
16 The boy is eager to please.
17 The boy is certain to please.
18 It is easy/*eager/*certain to please the boy.
19 The boy is eager/*easy/*certain. He intends to please someone.
20 It is certain/*easy/*eager the boy will please.

In phonology, linguists have concerned themselves with such problems as the nature of the relationship of the stop consonants within 21 and of the vowels within 22:

21 pin, bin, spin
22 bit, beet, beer

Concern with such phenomena is not new in linguistics but the proposed solutions to phonological problems in terms of ordered rules and distinctive features are new. New also is a concern for the phonological rules which are required to establish relationships not between vowel pairs such as those in 23 but between vowel pairs such as those in 24:

23 beet and bit; bait and bet; boot and good

24. meter and metric; sane and sanity; phone and phonic; type and typical

Phonetic relationships certainly exist between the members of the pairs in 23, but linguists now regard the *phonological* relationships between the members of the pairs of related words in 24 as more important.

In semantics, the concern is with such matters as the acceptability or grammaticality of sentences such as 25-28:

25 The tree barked.
26 Our pet goldfish passed away yesterday.
27 John is as sad as the movie I saw.
28 Be intelligent!

These sentences have a variety of semantic and syntactic problems associated with them, some of which linguists and philosophers have begun to tackle only very recently.

It is apparent, then, that today insights are available into the English language that were not available a few years ago. These insights are generated by the theory of generative-transformational grammar. In a sense they are artifacts of that theory and are *correct* only in the sense that they conform to the requirements of the theory. It may well be that theories themselves are neither correct nor incorrect: theories are more interesting or less interesting rather than correct or incorrect. They are more interesting or less interesting because of the questions they raise and the answers they suggest to these questions. Unless theories continue to raise questions and provide insights, they become shop-worn and valueless. Today we see the linguistic theories of the 1940's in such a light. We tend to forget that they too were once new and bright, and also that "Bliss was it in that dawn to be alive."

What is available to language teachers today from linguistics are new insights into language, but insights which are theoretical artifacts at the same time. They cannot, however, be ignored, but must somehow be incorporated into teaching. The sets of sentences 1-10 probably suggest a new principle of gradation, that is of ordering structures from simple to complex. However, sentences 11 and 12 suggest that the criterion of frequency of usage demands that 12 be taught first rather than 11, except, of course, one must assume that if the theory is in some sense "correct," an understanding of 12 presupposes a knowledge of 11. Even though utterances 13-14 show us that ambiguity is an important aspect of language and must be accounted for, we must still note that most utterances are not ambiguous in context. Sentences 15-20 again alert us to ambiguity and the collapsing of many deep structures into but a few surface structures; however, one cannot help but wonder whether some of the solutions linguists propose are not pseudo-grammatical in nature. The phonological examples in 21-24 remind us that both competence and performance are important. Sentences 25-28 suggest that we never forget we are teaching the language to human beings who have lived and who have brains, and not to mindless machines hidden in dark basements.

Generative-transformational theory provides language teachers with new insights into language. For example, no one can read Jacobs and Rosenbaum's *English Transformational Grammar* (1968) and Langendoen's *Essentials of English Grammar* (1970) without being impressed by the insights into English structure that they contain. However, neither these grammars nor other existing descriptions provide teachers with any way of teaching these insights nor do they provide them with any way of assigning some kind of truth value to the insights on an absolute scale. Generative-transformational theory does provide a new metalanguage, a new zest, and new possibilities. However, the first two are no substitute for the last, and very little has been done so far to exploit the last. Some such exploitation of possibilities is necessary. At the moment there is a great deal of speculation about possibilites, but little actual experimentation has been done. The claims for success that have been made appear to be more colored by the newness and zest just mentioned, that is by the well-known Hawthorne effect, rather than by any intrinsic value. Noam Chomsky (1966) himself has expressed skepticism about the immediate usefulness to language pedagogy of the linguistic theory associated with him.

Rigorous experimentation is required in deriving principles of gradation in both syntax and phonology; serious study is demanded of the possibilities of using generative-transformational theory in contrastive analysis; urgent clarification is required of the still muddy concepts of competence and performance; and careful documentation is essential in the area of putative linguistic universals. The time has come for the serious work of consolidation if generative-transformational theory is to have some widespread and lasting influence in teaching English as a second language.

PSYCHOLOGY AND LANGUAGE TEACHING

Just as there has been a revolution in linguistics in the last decade so there has also been comparable turmoil in psychology in general and learning psychology in particular. At the time the audiolingual method was in its heyday, it drew upon insights both from linguistics and from learning theory, particularly from behavioristic psychology in one form or another. Specific responses were taught in relation to specific stimuli, students were taught to make appropriate responses to a variety of stimuli, habits were established, principles were acquired inductively, and reinforcement was offered in various forms, both intrinsic and extrinsic, natural and artificial. There was no particular reason for using linguistic insights within one learning theory rather than within another. Practitioners usually try to use current insights from relevant disciplines and this is what happened in language teaching. In retrospect, we can see that it would have been equally possible to have used insights from structural linguistics with other varieties of learning theory. By historical accident they came to be associated with various versions of behavioristic theory. The clearest account of such linking of behavioristic learning theories to second language teaching is contained in Wilga Rivers' *The Psychologist and the Foreign Language Teacher* (1964).

Today, we have additional versions of learning theory available to us and are aware of the multitude of factors that must be taken into account. However, it would be well to note Carroll's comment that "available psychological theories are a long way from dealing with the complexities of language behavior, particularly its grammatical features" (1966a). We must still work within a theory and, in a very real sense, the theory defines the data, just as the kind of spectacles we wear determines both what we see and how we see it. Today, psychologists are concerned with such matters as innateness, learning preferences and styles, cognition, cognitive structures, and sociological as well as psychological factors in learning. Therefore, any approaches to teaching English as a second language which are likely to convince teachers of their validity must take cognizance of such emphases, and simplistic theories of conditioning, or even sophisticated theories of conditioning, will appear to be quite unconvincing. And, if teachers are not convinced that what they are doing is somehow right, what they are doing is not likely to work if only for that reason.

Considerable evidence now exists that different people learn in different ways and that such learning preferences are as important in second-language learning as they are anywhere else. Students learn through the eye as well as through the ear, by deduction as well as by induction, and by learning *about* as well as by learning *how*. There is little reason to believe that the order listen, speak, read, and write is sacrosanct in second-language acquisition, or that inductive learning is more efficient than deductive learning. Particularly this is the case when we are dealing with older children and adults who have *learned to learn* in certain ways. Although these ways may not always be very efficient, they certainly cannot be ignored nor dismissed out of hand. There are many ways to learn that *dog* refers to a certain kind of animal or that *jump* refers to a certain kind of action: one can touch dogs, look at pictures of dogs, translate *Hund* or *chien* from another language; one can jump and say "jump" together, look at real people jumping, look at pictures of people jumping; and so on. There is little reason to believe that *dog* and *jump* must be learned in one way rather than in another. It may of course be desirable to teach as much of the language as possible in context. For other reasons, however, it is doubtful that most learning situations can provide any more than a very limited and skewed set of contexts for language use.

Learning theorists are also concerned with cognitive development in one form or another. They seek to know how cognitive abilities develop and they are interested in how learners "use their brains" in learning. In second-language learning there is a consequent emphasis on developing the same ability to talk about the world in the second language as exists in the first language. Just as ability in the first language is structured in various ways, so the task in second-language teaching is one of introducing a corresponding structure for the second language: to teach time relationships, aspects, honorifics, pronominal systems, and so on. Learning theorists also want students to give conscious attention to tasks when such attention seems appropriate so that the teaching and learning can be made more effective: tense systems can be explained and related to various time dimensions; aspectual distinctions can be discussed and paraphrases offered in the native language; and the subtleties of honorifics and pronominal systems can be described. For each of these there can be both discussion *and* practice. This whole approach is not unattractive to language teachers, and a type of language learning theory which has been called *cognitive-code learning* theory has come into vogue in some circles. Psychologically, it appears to be well justified, but until more is known about the specific details of the English code, that is how English works, for example in its tense, aspectual, and pronominal systems, what success such a theory has may derive as much from the enthusiasm it arouses in its devotees as from any psychological or linguistic validity.

Psychologists are also aware that both language and learning are in some sense social phenomena. Language both holds together and divides mankind. Styles of learning also vary widely among cultures. In certain parts of the world, second, third, and even fourth or fifth languages "come easily" to everyone; in other societies a second language is "difficult" for anyone to acquire. Then again certain things must be learned at certain times and in certain ways in different cultures, whether these are courtship patterns, industrial skills, or additional languages. In North America the first are learned from peers, the second in the world of work, and the third in schools. The pattern may be quite different in other societies where either different divisions of labor exist or where entirely different groups may assume the role of teacher. One of the most interesting recent discussions of some of these problems is contained in *Styles of Learning Among American Indians: An Outline for Research* (Center for Applied Linguistics, 1969). In dealing with very differently oriented groups, we should be aware of the psychological difficulties our students may encounter in learning English because of the particular setting in which we do the teaching, or of our age, or sex, or social status. Any one of these factors, and a number besides, can negate teaching which would otherwise be successful.

Two other important concerns of psychologists should find a place in the thinking of anyone involved in second-language teaching. These are the concerns with any differences that might exist between first- and second-language acquisition on the one hand, and with the nature of bilingualism on the other hand. It is possible to make some observations about differences between first- and second-language learning, for example the universality of the former but not of the latter, the apparent drastic decrease in second-language learning ability which occurs during adolescence, the availability of cognitive strategies in second-language learning, and so on. However, little that has been written on the topic can be characterized as anything more than speculative. The evidence on types of bilingualism (*coordinate*, in which the two languages function independently, and *compound*, in which one language acts as a mediator for the other) is only a little more convincing.

Carroll (1966b) has pointed out that the ferment in psychology is very much like that in linguistics. The main difference is that there seem to be more uncertainties within psychology, or within the part that is of special interest to language teachers, because learning psychology has not fallen as strongly under the spell of a single theory as has linguistics. More options seem to be available in learning theory than in linguistics. However, we should note in all fairness that certain generative-transformationalists have expressed a serious interest in psychological matters because they claim to be interested in the human mind. They regard linguistics as part of cognitive psychology and matters of both perception and cognition interest them deeply. Since the psychology they espouse is cognitive rather than behavioristic, it is likely that some kind of union of generative-transformational grammar and cognitive psychology will result. The exact form of the union is still uncertain, but it is likely to influence second-language teaching for many years to come.

LANGUAGE TEACHING PEDAGOGY

Much of the concern in second-language teaching has been with either the type of linguistic knowledge that must be taught or theories of learning. Quite often much less consideration has been given to actual teaching techniques and classroom practices. It would even be true to say that many such techniques and practices have been imported into teaching from other disciplines. Linguists and psychologists have used certain techniques in their work and language teachers have tended to adopt and adapt these same techniques, as for example the use of minimal pairs, discrimination tasks, stimulus-response drills, and so on. Some of these same techniques lent themselves very well to use with audio-visual devices, of which the tape recorder and language laboratory have been the most conspicuous. In recent years some disenchantment has arisen with both the techniques and "hardware" such as the language laboratory when various inadequacies appeared: a useful technique in linguistic analysis is not necessarily a useful technique for teaching a grammatical point; a language is anything but a simple system of stimuli and accompanying responses; and the language laboratory is a poor substitute for a live teacher, although it is better than no teacher at all and possibly better than a bad teacher.

In recent years there has been some concern in pedagogy for either programing materials in some way or in spiraling materials. Programing requires a very detailed analysis of what has to be taught and of terminal behavior, so it is difficult to see how a course in English as a second language can be programed. Spiraling allows for growth and for uncertainty, and it recognizes a gradually developing control of various kinds of structures rather than mastery of structures item by item. As yet, materials and programs in teaching

English as a second language seem to favor the programing approach; perhaps more emphasis should be placed on spiraling, as in recent books by Lawrence (1972) and Morley (1972). More emphasis should also be placed on a wider variety of instructional techniques and settings than those that presently concern the teacher, particularly in courses which claim to be intensive, for otherwise such courses may tend to become very monotonous.

Language teaching publications describe numerous teaching methods. Perhaps it is also time for the notion of method to be given close examination. Attempts such as that made by Mackey in his *Language Teaching Analysis* (1965) to describe the variables involved in discussing methodology are welcome, but any examination of Mackey's book will indicate how far we must still go in specifying all the components of any method. Obvious difficulties exist with assessing methods, with classroom experimentation, with data collection on the incidence of certain problems, and with testing any kind of innovation.

LINGUISTICS, PSYCHOLOGY, AND PEDAGOGY

The preceding discussion reveals some of the uncertainty that exists about how a second language should be taught. The results of classroom experiments also tend to be inconclusive, as reported for example in Scherer and Wertheimer's *A Psycholinguistic Experiment in Foreign-language Teaching* (1964), or of limited application, as for example in dissertations by McKinnon (1965), Lim (1968), and Hauptman (1970). There are various claims and counterclaims but little certainty. Some theorists would insist on placing more emphasis on linguistic explanation, others on making more use of deductive teaching, and still others on giving greater recognition to the contexts of linguistic communication. However, more emphasis on explanation and deduction can lead right back to situations in which students learn a great deal about another language but cannot use it, and more emphasis on context and communication can reduce the possibility of any kind of systematic instruction. The safest course is perhaps the eclectic one in which the individual teacher uses what is best wherever he finds it and refuses to subscribe to a single narrow dogma. Perhaps a new method will develop which will achieve the same kind of general approval as the audiolingual method, but at the moment there is no consensus as to what it would be like, nor does there exist anywhere a body of principles which might form its basis.

chapter eleven
Linguistics, Psychology, and Pedagogy

What should a teacher engaged in teaching English to speakers of other languages know of linguistics, of psychology, and of pedagogy? How much does each of these three disciplines contribute to the others in an overall teaching methodology? Are they perhaps quite separate with nothing at all to contribute to each other? May not any unity we find be in reality a forced one, a marriage of convenience (à trois, of course), or a rationalization of existing practice rather than a theoretically valid unity? Do we have a *trinity* or a *unity*? These questions are particularly important at this time because the three disciplines themselves are in a state of change: linguistics is filled with controversy concerning the proper goals of linguistic endeavor; learning psychology is apparently moving away from studies of rats in mazes and of pigeons in boxes to computer simulation of behavior and to studies of electrical, chemical, and neurophysiological functioning; and pedagogy is concerned more and more with content, with strategies of learning, and with the structuring of knowledge.

However, even in this apparent disunity in the disciplines there is a very remarkable kind of unity. Each of the disciplines is reverting to types of inquiry which certain former practitioners pursued. In current linguistics, Chomsky has looked so far into the past for historical antecedents to his interests in linguistic theory and language acquisition that he has even been called a "neomedieval philosopher" by one of his critics (Hockett, 1967, p.144). In current psychology, there is a return to some of the concerns of early psychologists such as reasoning and the genesis of ideation, and no longer is the inside of the "black box" forbidden territory. In current educational thought, there has been a noticeable return to a kind of neo-pragmatism, to a "John Dewey with a hard nose" approach (*Saturday Review*, December 16, 1967). However, this kind of unity (or disunity) is not the kind which will be discussed here. Instead, the purpose is to show that in each historical period an attempt is made, conscious or otherwise, to unite the prevailing knowledge of language, the prevailing understanding of language learning, and the prevailing concept of educational goals into a pattern of language teaching. Such a pattern may actually be said to represent the best thought of its time and demonstrates the "conventional wisdom" of its period. It would, of course, be quite untrue to say that such a pattern is universally subscribed to in its period, for apparently there has never been a time when one pattern of second-language teaching existed to the exclusion of all others.

At the risk of oversimplification the patterns for each of three historical periods will be characterized as the *prelinguistic* pattern, the *linguistic* pattern, and the *contemporary* pattern. The word *characterize* is deliberately used, for at any one time we can characterize our own discipline both as it exists at that time and as it seems to have existed at other times. Such characterizations may be myths, but they are no less important for that in that they provide us with a foundation or rationale on which to base our teaching.

THE PRELINGUISTIC PATTERN

In the years immediately before, and to some extent during, the beginnings of modern linguistic science, there was, in the school rooms at least, a confusion of speech and writing, a belief in the appropriateness of a universal Latinate grammatical model for all languages, and no real search for theories which might account for the complexities of a natural language. In psychology the emphasis was on such concepts as the association of ideas, mental discipline, overlearning, memory and forgetting. It is not surprising then that when the educated élite of the period prized the classics and placed great value on encyclopedic formal knowledge, the prevailing pedagogy in second-language teaching should have been one which emphasized grammar-translation, learning *about* a language rather than learning a language, and reading and writing rather than listening and speaking. There were strong undercurrents of dissent from such emphases, but they were no more than that. Anyone wishing to choose representative books for the prelinguistic pattern need go no further than that phrase book which contains the foreign language equivalents of such an expression as "The postillion has been struck by lightning" or the famous Coleman Report (1929) with its claims about the desirability of teaching students to read foreign languages rather than to speak them.

One point deserves special mention: languages were often taught quite successfully in this period. The goals set out for language teaching were probably achieved quite regularly by those teachers who believed in what they were doing. These goals certainly differed from the goals we have today, but that is quite another matter. We must also presume that the teachers did find a unity among linguistics, psychology, and pedagogy and that they could justify what they were doing either in terms of stating a set of principles on which their practices were based, hence *a priori*, or in terms of a rationalization to justify practice, hence *a posteriori*.

THE LINGUISTIC PATTERN

The linguistic pattern is more relevant to us than the prelinguistic pattern, for it was the pattern of the period in which many of us were trained, and it is that training we bring to our work today. However, the students we are training today are almost certainly going to be working in a period which will be quite different.

In the period dominated by the linguistic pattern of second-language teaching, the study of language became more "objective" because the prevailing scientific viewpoint in language study valued dispassionate observation of data. The period also witnessed important attempts to wrestle with the implications of various distinctions: for example, the speech-writing distinction and the Saussurean *langue-parole* distinction. There was also a widespread belief that a linguist could describe any language through either the postulation or discovery of its significant units, contrasts, and patterns. This characterization needs little further amplification, for it is very familiar.

A similar familiarity undoubtedly exists with the prevailing psychology, which became more "scientific" and "experimental." There was an interest in the "laws" of learning (à la Thorndike) and in the concepts of transfer and interference. Watsonian behaviorism and Skinnerian reinforcement reigned, but occasionally the voice of the Gestaltists could be heard. In psychology the period was one in which psychologists emphasized habit formation, induction, and transfer (both positive and negative), and they too, like linguists, ruled the inside of the head almost entirely out of bounds as a legitimate area of concern.

When the pressures of war and international involvement made it necessary to teach second languages to large numbers of students in situations which enabled their teachers to employ subtle forms of coercion, a new unity was found. It is not surprising that this unity reflected the kind of linguistic, psychological, and pedagogical interests just mentioned. Just as it is possible to choose a phrase book and the Coleman Report as representative works of the prelinguistic period, it is possible to choose a similar representative work for the linguistic period. Lado's book *Language Teaching* (1964) is just such a work, for it is a deliberate attempt to formalize in extremely simple terms the prevailing views of linguistics and of psychology, and to integrate these into a statement about pedagogy. However, it could equally well. be argued that Lado's statement about language teaching is a rationalization or justification of a set of practices that had grown up unsystematically and accidentally rather than a rigorous statement of axioms and derivative practices. The book is actually a rather simple statement which characterizes the practices of the 1950's and tries to give them a theoretical base. As a characterization it offered teachers a rationalization for what they were doing and a justification for the use of such technological innovations as language laboratories and teaching machines. Lado's book offers an account of language teaching which possesses all the advantages of a characterization, for it is economical, clear, and simple; however, at the same time it has all the disadvantages since it is really a statement of belief and therefore probably unassailable and invulnerable.

THE CONTEMPORARY PATTERN

When we turn from the linguistic period to the contemporary scene in linguistics, psychology, and pedagogy in order to discover what each of these disciplines is like today, we must likewise look for evidence of disunity or unity. Are we still subscribers to the point of view formalized by Lado? If we are not, what characterization do we have to substitute for Lado's? What are we saying or what do we intend to say to the next generation of language teachers, that generation which is actually in our classrooms today seeking answers from us?

First of all, linguistics as a discipline has undergone a tremendous change in the last decade, a change of the kind that Kuhn in *The Structure of Scientific Revolutions* (1962) has called a revolution. The goals of the discipline as pursued by Chomsky, Fillmore, the Lakoffs, and others are vastly different from those of Bloomfield, Trager, and Hockett, and the problems that interest them are also different. This statement is not meant to be a criticism of the interests of structural linguists, for linguistics is certainly a big enough discipline to include widely diverging interests. Today, the major thrust in contemporary linguistics is toward an exploration of the formal characteristics of grammatical models and an understanding of the subtle interplay of syntax and semantics. There are also far different claims made today than a decade ago about what it means to *know* a language and to *acquire* a language even though these problems are usually discussed only in relation to first-language acquisition, with second-language acquisition scarcely mentioned.

In psychology, too, there have been great changes. Just as linguists have disputed the proper goals of linguistics, so have psychologists disputed the proper goals of psychology. One result of such dispute has been rather less observation of lower animals and rather more emphasis on understanding the processes of perception, cognition, and learning, that is on understanding the higher mental processes. Psychologists, too, are attempting to model the inside of the head and to simulate human capabilities in order to gain a better understanding of cognitive structures, categorizing abilities, and information transmission, and of the various strategies and plans that an organism has available or can acquire. Even the postulation of innate structures and properties is found to be quite acceptable. In education, too, there is a return to the organization of knowledge, to the self-discipline of learning, and to the range of individual variation in interests and abilities.

One result of all this activity is that the so-called linguistic method of language teaching is under severe attack from various sides. Several of the criticisms are worthy of comment. Speaking of the wartime language schools, Roberts (Wilson, 1967) wrote:

> If you put a bright young soldier into a room with a native speaker of Japanese and keep them there eight hours a day for eighteen months, the soldier will learn quite a lot of Japanese, even if his text is just a Japanese translation of Cicero and his instructor is a nitwit. Unless, of course, the soldier simply goes mad, which also happened now and then (p. xxvii).

There is considerable truth in Roberts' statement. The linguistic method worked in many cases but other methods also worked. The really interesting questions are: "Why does a method work, and why does it work very well at one time but not well at all at another time?" A second comment comes from Robert Politzer (1967) at the conclusion of a report on an experiment in which various combinations of drill and explanation were compared:

In conclusion we point out that the independent variable under investigation—place of or absence of explanation—does perhaps not have the importance attributed to it in some of the current pedagogical discussion. That class differences (even with classes taught by the same teacher!) turned out to be more significant than treatment differences is an indication that in the actual practical teaching situation the Foreign Language teacher should indeed pay a great deal of attention to such variables as the time of meeting of the class, the degree of eagerness or tiredness of the student at certain times of the day, etc. As many Foreign Language teachers have no doubt suspected for some time, such variables may, in the long run, make at least as much of a difference as some of the refinements of teaching methodology.

Politzer's comment brings us a little closer to a full awareness of the complexity of the problem of understanding exactly which variables are important in language learning. Perhaps we should be a little more honest than we are and admit that we do not really know how people learn. At best we can make only more or less satisfactory guesses, and these guesses account for parts only of the language-learning process.

The third statement is a claim about language learning and language teaching by Bull (1965):

Learning to talk like a Spaniard means first to think like a Spaniard. This book is dedicated to the proposition that it is easier to learn to think like a Spaniard if the teacher can explain how a Spaniard thinks (p. 18).

This claim is very strong indeed: we should teach Spanish by teaching the thought processes of Spaniards. The claim suggests that a lot is known about these processes. On the contrary, we know next to nothing about these processes and the claim is spurious. The book in which it is made also seems to suggest that somehow a generative-transformational grammar of Spanish offers some kind of characterization of the thought processes of Spanish-speakers. Again this claim is spurious. Still another instance of a similar kind of claim comes from a paper presented by Diller at the Tenth International Congress of Linguists in Bucharest in 1967:

In sum ... generative grammarians would agree that a language is learned through an active cognitive process rather than through an externally imposed process of conditioning and drill. Further, they would agree that grammatical rules are psychologically real and that people must use these rules— consciously or not—in speaking or understanding a language.

N. Chomsky (1966) himself has given us the following very clear warning about such claims:

I am, frankly, rather skeptical about the significance, for teaching of languages, of such insights and understanding as have been attained in linguistics and psychology ... [and] ... suggestions from the 'fundamental disciplines' must be viewed with caution and skepticism (p. 43).

We must heed Chomsky's warning if we are to resist the stampede in this contemporary period of language teaching toward the adoption of a new pedagogy in which the new linguistics, the new psychology, and the new demands made of our. educational system will find themselves welded into a new unity which will have *no more theoretical justification than any past unity*.

TOWARD UNITY

This last statement obviously requires a defense. When we look at the prelinguistic pattern, we can now see that there was really little or no reason for the particular unification of linguistic, psychological, and pedagogical understandings that occurred. We can make the same statement for the linguistic pattern. Other views of linguistics, psychology, and education existed in addition to those that found their way into the linguistic method. However, the kind of unity that the method provided did give its practitioners an approach or rationale within which to work. As Anthony (1963) has pointed out, an approach is axiomatic so that it is by definition beyond proof or disproof. An approach is a matter of belief, and the beliefs on which the linguistic method was based came from many sources. Sometimes an approach is based on axioms or beliefs, but sometimes too axioms and beliefs are developed in an apparent attempt to justify existing methods. Perhaps we would do well to examine the linguistic method in detail to see if it is not an instance of this latter process of justification. Today, though, the system of beliefs associated with the linguistic method is held by a declining number of the key people in second-language teaching. Many of the others are engaged in formalizing a new approach which will be based on the beliefs that they find acceptable today. But while they seek to formulate a set of axioms, actual teaching innovations are occurring in the classrooms. Gradually there will be a merging of theory and practice, and *ipso facto* a new unity will emerge. This will happen, but it has not yet happened.

There is though a puzzle in this process. We do not need to have a new unity in the contemporary period because it is intrinsically better than either of the previous unities. In fact, it is impossible to test for *better* or *worse* in this sense. We need a new unity for an entirely different reason. *We need a new unity in order to reflect our current characterization of the basic disciplines and to justify what we are doing in classrooms.* We need it so that we can feel that our practice is theoretically justified and so that we can be properly committed to what we are doing. At the moment many of our younger teachers feel rather insecure. They find the linguistic method quite unacceptable since it employs the wrong rhetoric. They cannot believe in it; consequently, the method will not work for them. But they have nothing with which to replace it, for there is no new rhetoric available. For them there is no self-fulfilling prophecy which says that to make something work you must believe in it, and, if you believe in something, it will work for you.

The next generation of teachers of English to speakers of other languages must find an approach to their work which will serve them as well as the linguistic method served its believers. It is not possible to agree entirely with Hayes (1966) when he wrote:

> [Teachers] must sómehow cease to regard 'methods' as matters of 'belief,' while learning to understand and to question the assumptions underlying suggested approaches (p. vi).

We must certainly train teachers to question, but they must also believe in what they are doing. They must avoid blind unquestioning belief, but teachers need to believe in something in order to succeed in their teaching. One of the greatest challenges we have before us as teacher-trainers is to help our trainees articulate a set of beliefs which will allow them to be as successful as we have been, but which at the same time gives them the opportunity to grow and change as the theoretical advances in linguistics, psychology, and pedagogy continue. It is a challenge which should demand the fullest attention of everyone engaged in teacher training.

chapter twelve
From Theory to Practice

It is useful from time to time to attempt to relate the theory of teaching English as a second language to some current practices in teaching English as a second language so as to bridge the gap between the practical orientation of teachers and the theoretical concerns that should underlie practice. Theory can never be ignored in discussions of classroom practices, because good practices must necessarily derive from good theory. Every classroom practice derives from adequate or good knowledge of language, psychology, and pedagogical philosophy; every bad practice gives evidence of some or other weakness in our understanding of language, psychology, or pedagogy.

In building, or at least attempting to build, a bridge between practice and theory, we must necessarily discuss what some of the problems are in each of these three disciplines and decide how solutions to these problems have certain consequences for classroom practice. It may also be interesting to relate any conclusions to a paper by Anthony (1963), in which he discussed the differences between *approach*, *method*, and *technique* in second-language teaching and the necessity for insisting on the priority of approach over method, and, in turn, of method over technique.

LINGUISTICS

First of all, what are some of the current problems in the discipline of linguistics as that discipline bears on problems of language teaching and language learning? One of the very first problems is that of coming to an understanding of the nature of language itself. While all linguists acknowledge that a language is a system of some kind, they tend to disagree among themselves as to how that system should be characterized and what its total scope should be. Is it, for example, a system which may be expressed in a set of rules, or in a set of patterns, or in some other special kinds of grammatical category? Should the system merely describe or characterize a set of sentences which the linguist has happened to observe, possibly a very large set, or should it characterize the set of all possible sentences, a set that the linguist has no possible hope of ever observing because it is infinite? Even if linguists agree that a language is a system which may be expressed in the form of rules, they may well disagree about the "reality" of the rules a particular linguist writes. Are the rules he writes in his grammar psychologically real; that is do they somehow also exist in a speaker's and a listener's minds, or are they merely an artifact of the linguist's descriptive process? It is certainly true to say that in many cases a great deal of confusion exists about the terms *rule* and *rule of grammar*, and it is well to be on the alert for potential confusion in the use of these terms.

Linguists will also tend not to be in complete agreement about what the discipline of linguistics is all about. Some will say that linguistics is really a search for language universals, those linguistic characteristics which may be found in all languages; others will say that linguistics is a search for methods of analysis; still others will be concerned with making language descriptions, particularly descriptions of exotic languages, on a largely *ad hoc* basis. The result of such different emphases, of course, are very different kinds of linguistic interests, varying according to the particular linguist one reads or listens to, and very different kinds of understandings about the discipline of linguistics itself. Therefore, it is not surprising that a variety of views exists as to what a grammar is. Is a grammar a theory about both language in general and one language in particular; or is a grammar no more than a description of one language; or is a grammar simply some kind of demonstration that a particular linguistic system is workable? Then, even given some measure of agreement about what language is, what linguistics is about, what a grammar is or should be, linguists may well still disagree about whether actual language use is a *skill* which is largely *habitual* or an *ability* which is largely *creative*. Is language use a skill which can be learned much as one learns to type, or is it an ability like walking, which is acquired in an entirely different way from typing skill? Everyone learns to walk but not everyone learns to type. And everyone learns to talk, too. There do appear to be some critically important differences which must be recognized.

When we turn our attention to second-language learning and examine it in the light of what linguists believe a language and grammar to be, we must ask ourselves what must be learned. Is it a system of abstract rules, or a system of habits, or a set of general principles? Or is it a collection of specific items, for example "sentences" or "patterns," which are then manipulated by the second-language learner in ways that we do not well understand? Most linguists will admit that they really do not know much at all about what must be learned when a second language must be acquired.

This kind of overview of the discipline of linguistics suggests that many unanswered questions remain. In fact, linguists are currently more concerned with formulating questions than with proposing answers. A healthy attitude toward this state of affairs would be to accept it as a sign of the good health of the discipline, for it indicates the likelihood of major new advances, not of decay and dissolution. It is also possible to see some of the results of this kind of concern for formulating interesting questions by looking at certain very specific linguistic concepts which have existed for many years. For example, the concept of the phoneme has been with us for several decades. This concept has always been a controversial one in linguistics and it is just as controversial today as it was a decade or two ago. However, today the controversies relate to an entirely different set of problems: they now relate to the connection between meaning and sound within an overall language system rather than to such problems as neutralization and overall system, which plagued linguistics for so long. Then, again, the distinction between a class of words called *verbs* and another called *adjectives*, which seems to be such a simple and obvious distinction, has been called into question by some linguists who believe that verbs and adjectives are really the same kind of word. They claim that adjectives behave very much like verbs and that there are really only basically three types of words: noun-like words, verb-like words, of which adjectives are a sub-group, and a set of relational words, which do not have any propositional or referential content and therefore function quite differently from the other two types. There are many such problems one could discuss: the current concern with the place of meaning in linguistic analysis and linguistic description; the concern with various kinds of abstract syntactic processes; and the concern with the relationship of meaning to syntax, and of meaning and syntax together to phonology. In all of these areas the student of linguistics will see many questions asked, for linguistics is in a state of rapid development, quick changes, and great excitement. However, he will find few answers.

At this point we may ask how such facts as these influence what teachers should do in their classrooms. How do current concerns in linguistic theory bear on classroom practices? First of all, students still have to learn certain things if they are to speak the second language, regardless of the state that theoretical linguistics finds itself in. For example, students who are learning English must still learn to distinguish *beet* from *bit*, *bait* from *bet*, and *bet* from *bat*. They must learn that in English those words which we may still want to refer to as *adjectives* go in front of nouns, and that subjects usually precede predicates. They must learn that adjectives do not agree in number with nouns. They must still learn that an animal which barks is called a *dog*, not a *Hund*, nor a *chien*, nor a *perro*. They must still learn what the acceptable sentence patterns of English are, even though these sentence patterns might be called *surface structures* and be somehow of less interest to theoretically-oriented linguists than something called *deep structures*. Our students must still learn that there are basic building blocks which they must be able to put together to make sense in the new language. They must still learn to speak by being required to do some speaking, for they cannot possible learn to speak only by thinking about speaking. Therefore, they need drill and they need practice. We cannot hope to inject students with some kind of abstract underlying structure in the hope that they will come out speaking English, some recent claims apparently to the contrary notwithstanding.

The discipline of linguistics is in a state of flux, and the questions being asked are extremely theoretical. However, we cannot teach English as a second language by teaching our students to understand the questions or some of the proposed answers. The students still need to hear dialogues; they still need to have expansion drills in which, given one part of a sentence, they add on another part, add then another part, and finally build up the complete sentence from the back to the front. Students need substitution drills in which they learn to deal with problems such as anaphora, that is the correct substitution of words like *it*, *one*, and other pronominals. They also need transformation exercises to practice changing one structure into another. It should be emphasized that *transformation* in this sense is not the transformation of the generative-transformational linguist. He uses that term in an entirely different way, so it is necessary to be on the alert for any possible confusion.

Now it is quite legitimate to ask, as many linguists do, what exactly a child is learning about language when he mimics dialogues, when he expands sentences, when he makes substitutions, and when he changes one sentence into another. We are surely not just teaching the child rote habits which are completely unproductive, as sometimes we are accused. We are sometimes also accused of stifling his creativity, or, less severely, of not recognizing the fact that language use is a creative activity, and that creativity cannot be encouraged or even initiated by the kinds of exercises we employ. However, those who have criticized such practices have not yet demonstrated how a learner can create a second language without stimuli, and they have not been afraid to use language stimuli in their own teaching which look rather like those many of us have been using for quite a long time. There is obviously a need for good stimuli in language teaching, and the kinds of exercises just mentioned (mimicry, expansion, substitution, and transformation) seem to be necessary in any kind of systematic second-language teaching. It would be entirely foolish to throw these overboard in order to sail the completely uncharted sea of creativity!

The last statements should not be interpreted as presenting a case for mindless pattern drill, blind mim-mem methods, and pattern practice *ad nauseam*. The learner does make a large contribution in language learning and linguists have very rightly stressed that contribution in any kind of language learning. However, it must in all fairness be pointed out that linguists are uncertain what the contribution is, even though they are quite certain that it does exist. A learner always knows certain things about another language before he learns it. For example, he knows that certain kinds of phonological contrasts will occur, that there will be naming and action words, and that there will be sentences which have definite structures to enable him to make statements, give commands, and ask questions. Of course, children cannot verbalize such under-standings, but it is fair to assume that they do have them nevertheless. Our linguistic knowledge would suggest that when a student learns a second language he is aware that both meaning and structure are involved in the learning and that there is a critical relationship between the context in which the language is used and the structure of the language which is used in that context. No one can learn a language in a vacuum in which the sounds he hears are unconnected to events in the real world, just as no one can learn a language without having actual linguistic data presented to him. Linguistic theory tells us that we should not forget the *context* of language learning. Linguistic theory suggests that we cannot rely exclusively on mimicry, dialogues, mim-mem methods, and pattern-practice drill, and ignore actual language use and the contexts in which language is used. Nor should we go to the opposite extreme of following a method, like the direct method, in which linguistic structure is almost totally ignored. Our classroom practices should follow some kind of middle road, some kind of strategy in which the natural contexts of language are employed to prompt the use of the language structures which must be mastered.

PSYCHOLOGY

Turning our attention to psychology, we discover many of the same problems that arose in considering the relevance of linguistic knowledge. Indeed, linguistics itself has been called a branch of cognitive psychology, because many of the same questions interest both linguists and psychologists. For example, both linguists and psychologists are interested in the basic question of what the human mind is like, and particularly, what the human mind must be like, given the kind of structures that languages have. Linguists ask what kinds of structures all languages have and what the universal characteristics of language are. Then they tend to speculate on what human minds must be like to be able to use such languages. Or they may speculate that human languages must be as they are as a result of the structure of human minds. While we can observe human languages in action, we cannot directly observe human minds in action because of a lack of sufficiently sophisticated equipment. Therefore, the study of language turns out to be one very interesting way of making hypotheses about the structure of human minds, and it is largely for this reason that linguistics has been referred to as a branch of cognitive psychology.

However, when we look at psychology in second-language teaching and learning, we are really less concerned with speculation about what human minds are like than with the problems of language learning. Language *learning* is emphasized rather than language *teaching*. It has been said, with some justification, that first languages are not taught: they are learned, for they are just too complicated to be taught. How can a parent, or a teacher for that matter, possibly teach something that even very sophisticated linguists hardly even begin to understand? In second-language learning and teaching the same problem exists. How can anyone teach a second language when so little is known about any one language and about almost every aspect of the learning process? It is necessary to assume that the learner makes a tremendous contribution in the process.

If so little is known about the structure of language, it seems difficult to explain how a second language can be learned through some of the simplistic psychological learning models that are available, through, for example, any kind of stimulus-response theory, that is through a theory in which a language is regarded as a simple habit system. Nor can that variation of behavioristic learning theory called reinforcement theory adequately describe or account for how a second language can be learned in its totality. Learning a second language means acquiring a system of rules, but just as very little is known about these rules, even less is known about how such rule systems are acquired. It is possible to argue about the relative effectiveness of deductive learning and inductive learning, but most of what has been said on this topic is speculative and has not been proved out in any rigorous manner. We can also make hypotheses about the influence of motivation on learning, of both extrinsic and intrinsic motivation. We can investigate different types of learning as these vary, for example, with the age or the sense preferences of the learner. We can inquire into the various halo effects associated with learning, those halo effects associated with the equipment we use, our materials, the time of day our class is held, the teacher's personality, and particular mixes of students. There are numerous psychological factors in any learning situation, and we really know very little about them.

There are certain data available on the learning process that do have special interest for us. One of the most interesting collections of such data is the evidence that linguistic interference provides. We know that students from certain linguistic backgrounds have difficulty in learning various aspects of English and that they do make predictable mistakes while learning. The Spanish student fails to distinguish *beat* and *bit* and *bait* and *bet*, and he does not pronounce *school* as *school* but as *eschool*. The Japanese student comes to study "the Engrish ranguage." Such mistakes, or deviations from an expected response, can tell us a lot, but not possibly as much as some have claimed. There was a time when contrastive analysis, that is the analysis of the two languages involved in second language learning and a statement of their contrasts, promised to work us miracles. The miracles never came. We should not abandon attempts at such analyses, but rather we should look at the unexpected responses in more fruitful ways than we have done in the past.

There are many problems then in psychology, and we are just beginning to ask interesting and answerable questions about them.

From what we do know already, we can suggest ways in which classroom practices might be modified and improved. One particular improvement would result from a change of emphasis from *teaching* to *learning*. Too often the classroom is regarded as a place in which the teacher is at the center of interest, a place in which everything flows from the teacher, who knows what is to be taught and exactly how he is going to teach it, and in which the learner is merely the end point of some kind of process. A change of direction seems called for, particularly if language is something that we understand but a little of and if any particular language is a system of which we have merely fragmentary knowledge. If our goal is somehow to help out students to acquire an adequate control of that second language, then the focus must be changed from the teacher to the *student*. Somehow we must realize that the student must do the job for himself, that we can help him, and that we can struggle with him in *his* task of learning the second language, but that since we know so little about that second language, we can provide little more than encouragement and a certain, but not unimportant, amount of help.

The emphasis, therefore, should be less on the teacher and the course or text and more on the student himself. We should stimulate him to use the language and encourage him to use his innate processes of language acquisition. Our methods must be eclectic rather than single-minded and monolithic. We cannot rely on any single narrow pedagogical approach. We must respond to the different needs of students, the different learning patterns they exhibit, and the different inclinations and motives that they have in learning. Obviously, in such a setting the teacher's role is less one of providing something absolutely sure and definitive, for such certainty does not exist, and more one of trying to create an atmosphere in which learning is encouraged, in which the teacher's enthusiasm for learning, desire for his students' success, and overall commitment to his task somehow rub off on his students. Consequently, there is a need for lots of examples, variety, and context-oriented work.

All of this may seem rather paradoxical, particularly if some of the preceding statements have been interpreted as meaning that we know nothing about language. We certainly do know many things about language, but not a few of these are superficial. For example, many of the phonological contrasts that we know about exist as phonetic contrasts, that is as actual contrasts in the stream of sound that comes out of the speakers' mouths, but not necessarily as contrasts at a more abstract level of language function. Many of the grammatical contrasts may be only surface contrasts existing in the sentences which are produced and may not be as significant as certain deep contrasts which interest linguists. These surface contrasts are still important in language use and, fortunately, we do know something about them. We must try to make sure that our students systematically acquire these same contrasts and some systematic approach to this task is possible. However, we should be more concerned with the student's gradual development as a person who controls a second language than with his apparent mastery of this pattern or that one. We *should attempt continually to find out what the student is doing with the language we are trying to teach him*. Our task is to help him to learn.

It is at this point that interference phenomena are so important. When a student does say something incorrectly, does not control a certain contrast, produces an ungrammatical sentence, does not know the right word, we should, in Newmark and Reibel's terms (1969), take this as evidence of his ignorance and incomplete learning. Linguistic interference is therefore linguistic ignorance. We should assume that the student is trying to use the second language, and, because he does not know enough, he is failing. The problem so far as pedagogy is concerned is that having recognized this as ignorance, how do we deal with it? Do we treat it through more drill or through explanation? The answer again is not a particularly simple one, because different people learn in different ways and variables like age and motivation are involved. It is quite possible that drill activities will work better with younger students, but in similar circumstances older students may prefer explanation. However, it is doubtful that one can explain the differences between the vowels in *beat* and *bit*: the tenseness of one vowel versus the laxness of the other; the off-glide of one versus the lack of glide of the other; and the height of one versus that of the other. The student must learn to hear the difference in the vowels and it is hard, if not impossible, to gain this ability from explanation alone. A grammatical point, however, may be explained, but explanation will not guarantee learning. Many of us know foreign students who know a lot *about* English but whose English is atrocious. Many of us know foreign students who speak beautiful English but do not know anything about English. In language teaching we must be prepared to mix drill and explanation because we can never be sure which technique works with which student.

PEDAGOGY

Pedagogy has been kept to the last in this discussion because it is true to say that even less is known about pedagogy than is known about linguistics and psychology. There is a classic question: "Is teaching an art or is it a science?" And also the question: "Can we examine the teaching process in any scientific manner?" No answer is proposed to either question, but there is evidence that teaching is an art and that the teaching process can also be studied scientifically. In second-language teaching much of what is discussed under teaching actually turns out to be a discussion of linguistics or of psychology. For example, it has long been fashionable to import into teaching certain techniques which linguists use in analyzing languages or in making language descriptions. The use of minimal pairs such as *beat-bit*, *bait-bet*, and *bet-bat* in language teaching seems to be an importation of a linguistic technique into the classroom. The same use may be seen of ideas from psychology: one way of explaining certain psychological phenomena is to hypothesize S-R bonds. Consequently, the teacher may attempt to import into the classroom a technique in which students are taught to associate certain stimuli with certain responses in a rather mechanical way. Again the result seems to be a direct extension into the classroom of a technique from another discipline.

Since pedagogy involves such matters as equipment as well as the content, we sometimes become fascinated by the "hardware" of education: audio-visual aids, language laboratories, overhead projectors, tape recorders, reading kits, and so on. Many of the pedagogical issues with which we become concerned center on such matters as whether or not to install a language laboratory, buy an overhead projector, or requisition one particular set of audio-visual aids. It is just such hardware that we show visitors to our school, that we insist on buying when we move into a new building, and that we fight the principal, curriculum supervisor, and school board for. And, rather tragically, it is just such hardware that ends up being quite underused once we have it. We install a beautiful language laboratory and we then cannot find suitable tapes to play at the master console. We equip our new school with a closed-circuit television system and then we cannot find the money to maintain it. We buy some elaborate equipment to use with programed materials and then we cannot find programed materials suitable for our students. We should resist the temptation to buy bigger and better hardware at the expense of the "software" of education, the actual content of teaching. The best hardware is chalk, a blackboard, and books, and the most valuable teaching aid in the classroom is a well-prepared teacher. We cannot solve all our classroom problems by employing more and more equipment, nor is the language laboratory the answer to all our needs in second-language teaching.

If we escape being hung up on hardware in pedagogy, we generally get hung up with techniques. For example, we may always insist that sounds and structures must be taught in contrast to each other. We may always insist on contrasting *l*'s with *r*'s, *e*'s with *i*'s and one grammatical structure with another. Or we may insist that we must have a particular kind of text for a particular kind of student: for example, specially oriented texts for various ethnic groups. Or we may insist that every new item must be repeated *n* times, the particular value of *n* itself varying from three to five or more. Or we may insist that whenever we present a new point, the presentation has to follow a certain order: preparation, presentation, consolidation, evaluation, review, and so on. Or we may have notions about simple and complex sounds and structures, notions with no more than an intuitive basis. Or we may insist on programing a certain grammatical sequence in a certain series of steps, again largely on an intuitive basis. Or we may believe in the effects of spiraling or cycling of our materials rather than in straightline programing.

Publishers cater to these preferences and advertise their offerings as much for the particular techniques they exemplify as for any intrinsic content. They sell us English through pictures, English through Basic English, English through drill, English through generative-transformational grammar, or English through portable transistorized receivers that can be plugged gently into the ear so that the learner can acquire English quite painlessly as he goes about his daily living and even daily sleeping. Teachers tend to accept this situation. We think our jobs will be easier if we have just the right texts, or if there is a language laboratory, or if we control a little teaching formula that will do the trick time and time again. Given the kinds of pressures that we work under in our classrooms, this result is not surprising.

Successful teaching does go on and we might seek to discover the reasons for success. One reason has to do with the learning environment. It is impossible to teach language in a sterile, inactive environment. Language is a vehicle for dealing with reality. All linguistic activity must be associated with meaningful activity, so any techniques designed to encourage meaningful activity are obviously important in language learning. Consequently, movement, involvement, and situation, and the concomitants of these—laughter, games, and stories—are important in teaching. Our teaching techniques should focus on encouraging as much of this as possible. Good pedagogy then will be less concerned with gimmickry, the pat solution, the utterly predictable lesson plan, and the rather dull teacher-centered activities of classrooms than with involving students and the teacher in some kind of jointly-meaningful activity in which the focus is on language learning rather than on language teaching. But we cannot forget the teacher. We should remember that he is extremely important, if only for the fact that he teaches not only the course that is prescribed, but also what *he himself is*, and what he is is usually learned much better by the students than any content he ever tries to communicate!

CONCLUSION

It would be useful to sum up this discussion of linguistics, psychology, and pedagogy, the three aspects of second language learning that we have to take into consideration, by referring to Anthony's terms *approach*, *method*, and *technique*.

By *approach* Anthony refers to the assumptions that underlie our language teaching, that is the assumptions we have about language and about psychology. He rightly says that such assumptions are generally matters of belief and are the axioms from which we derive the theorems, or the methods, and then the derivative techniques that we use. As classroom teachers, we should concern ourselves with the underlying axioms of our profession, because everything that we do in our classrooms derives from the assumptions we make. It does not matter whether or not we can articulate these assumptions; they are still there, articulated or not.

To Anthony *method* means the plans for curriculum and teaching which derive from approaches, the plans by which we ultimately present data. They are the plans for the curriculum of a particular kindergarten room in which there are Mexican-American children, or of a particular ghetto school, or of a small number of foreign students on a Midwest college campus, or of a special class for non-English-speaking students in a suburban school system. Method then is the particular kind of strategy that derives from an approach; it is the overall plan that we have in mind for teaching the language in a particular set of circumstances.

Technique, for Anthony, means exactly how we do what we

decide to do, that is the specific kinds of practices and techniques that are employed in a specific classroom. It is in this area of teaching that much of the interest of classroom teachers lies. We are all interested in becoming better classroom teachers. We all like to find something good and immediately useful in book displays at conventions. We all like to go away from professional meetings with at least one new practical idea that will work. But we would be doing a disservice to ourselves if all we do is hunt for gimmickry and new wrinkles, for example, a tape recorder with some new kind of switch, or a book which has appeared in a new cover, possibly even in a new edition, but really only the same poor old wine again. We should try instead, on occasion, to stand back from such concerns in order to achieve a perspective on our task and to evaluate our methods and our general approach.

Classroom teachers must be prepared to find out as much as they can about what the issues and questions are in linguistics and psychology in order to gain some idea of where the answers might lie. In the years ahead it will be more vital to understand what the basic questions are in the disciplines than it will be to understand what a certain switch does on the latest tape recorder, or how to use a particular set of flash cards, or what a very specific teaching technique will do in a rather limited set of circumstances. A teacher cannot get through a lifetime of teaching by throwing a succession of switches, or by using a collection of charts, or by inventing a new teaching wrinkle every day. Inevitably the result will be boredom or learning of the wrong things. However, he can take inspiration from a new idea about language teaching, from new sources of information, from new insights into the language-learning process, and from new ideas about what a total teaching strategy could be like. A good teacher probably should know how to use a tape recorder, an overhead projector, and some of the other media effectively, but a good teacher is not just a technician. A good teacher is someone who continually examines what he does, continually strives to arrive at new understandings of his discipline, and continually tries to steer a course between doubt and dogma. Good teaching practice is based on good theoretical understanding. *There is indeed nothing so practical as a good theory*. Teachers should focus from time to time not on techniques, not on methods, but on approach, that is on theory, and should try in those moments to capture some of the excitement of the many challenges that confront us in teaching English to speakers of other languages.

chapter thirteen
Teaching Structure

The teaching methodology we employ in classrooms usually reflects the knowledge we have of language structure and language function. Even the grammar-translation and direct methods of instruction are based on certain assumptions about language. In grammar-translation, for example, students are required to use whatever innate knowledge of languages they have to work out relationships between a particular pair of languages through a matching operation which focuses on meaning in a way which has never been made explicit. The great weakness of this method arises from the fact that it is quite inexplicit; in addition, it is almost invariably oriented toward writing rather than speaking, and it often becomes very boring in practice. In contrast, the direct method tends to be more lively and real than grammar-translation in that it deliberately focuses on the communicative function of language and on situations, apparently subordinating structure to communication whenever these come into conflict.

The emphasis we find today on linguistic structure in language teaching appears to have arisen from the discoveries of twentieth century linguists and their capture of key positions in the foreign-language-teaching profession, particularly during and shortly after the Second World War. A concern for either translation or cultural immersion was superseded by one for accounting for language as a system of contrasting sounds and structures, and for language learning as the mastery of a set of skills which comprise a habit system. A mastery of the contrasts between the two languages which were involved and of the contrasts within the target language itself was held to be critical in language learning, for example mastery of such contrasts as the phonetic ones between the English word *eel* and the French word *île*, and, within the English language, of the contrast between *ill* and *eel*. Allied to this view of language structure was a view of language learning which assumed that the new system should be established as a set of habits by various kinds of activities which would ensure overlearning. The results of these emphases was the linguistic method or audiolingual method of language teaching that came out of the pioneer work of linguists such as Charles Fries (1945).

However, all this is history. Today we find ourselves in possession of different notions about language, language structure, and language learning from those that were in the ascendancy as recently as the early 1960's. Today, too, we are looking for entirely new ways to teach what we know. In particular, ideas about language structure have changed considerably since the publication of *Syntactic Structures* (N. Chomsky, 1957). Now linguists tend to view language behavior as rule-governed creative behavior. They concern themselves with structures of two kinds, sometimes labeled deep and surface. They puzzle over ambiguity in meaning and structure, seek out paraphrase relationships among sentences, and search for the optimal system within which to characterize the abstract linguistic competence of some equally abstract ideal speaker-listener in a totally perfect speech environment. The theory demands such activity, so that is what linguists do. In considering the problems involved in language learning, they seek to explain what is meant by knowing a language, ask whether this knowledge can be taught (because no one really knows what it is), and make hypotheses about what a person must learn in acquiring a second language and what he does not need to learn. And, finally, they try to put everything together in the actual language teaching that goes on in classrooms.

A STRUCTURAL PROBLEM

Sentences 1 to 3 may be used to illustrate some of the problems just mentioned:

1 The boy is easy to please.
2 The boy is eager to please.
3 The boy is certain to please.

These sentences appear to have the "same" structure described in the formula given in 4:

4 NP BE Adjective Infinitive

Using a grammar-translation method of instruction, a teacher could ask students to relate the set of sentences 1 to 3 to the phonemically represented Persian set (5 to 7), or to the orthographically represented German set (8 to 10), if these were the first languages of his students:

5   /pesær-ra razi kæ dæn asan æst/

6   /pesær mostaque razi kædæn æst/

7   /hatmæn pesær razi mikonæd/

8   Der Junge ist leicht zufriedenzustellen.

9   Der Junge versucht elfrig, gefällig zusein.

10   Es ist sicher, dass der Junge gefällig sein wird.

Adopting a direct method of instruction, he could relate the English set to actual real life situations. In neither case would he teach the sets as *sets*, for there would be no reason to do so. Nor would he really be concerned about sentences 1 to 3 if the linguistic method of instruction were adopted, for on the surface these sentences have the identical structure indicated in 4 and he would scarcely be aware that a problem existed.

The reason for such an apparent oversight is obvious. It would scarcely occur to anyone working in the immediate pre-Chomskyan linguistic paradigm that the *easy*, *eager*, and *certain* examples formed an interesting linguistic problem. However, the Chomsky paradigm requires sentences 1 to 3 to be regarded as an interesting problem, because the one surface structure given in 4, apparently results from three different deep structures. There are three different deep structures because the relationships among *boy*, the three adjectives, and *please* are different in each example, a difference which is brought out in some of the paraphrases in 11 to 13, two variants 14 and 15 with quite different meanings, and in the deep structures which are mapped schematically in 16 to 18:

11   (a) What is easy to do is please the boy.

     (b) The boy pleases easily.

     (c) It is easy to please the boy.

     (d) Pleasing the boy is easy.

     (e) To please the boy is easy.

12   (a) What the boy is eager to do is please.

     (b) The boy's eagerness to please . . . .

     (c) The boy is eager.

13   (a) What the boy is certain to do is please.

     (b) The boy's certainty to please . . . .

     (c) That the boy will please is certain.

     (d) It is certain that the boy will please.

14 The boy is eager to be pleased.

15 The boy is certain to be pleased.

16

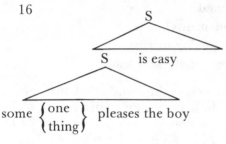

17

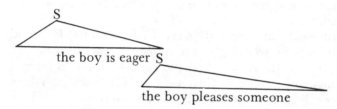

18

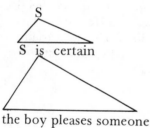

It is an artifact of generative-transformational theory that something like the deep structures shown in 16 to 18 must be considered to underlie sentences 11 to 13. The distinction among the deep structures in which *easy*, *eager*, and *certain* occur is, in a very important sense, forced by the grammatical model itself. However, it is also an undeniable linguistic observation that the actual sentences 1 to 3 look alike in a way that cannot be considered either uninteresting or trivial; consequently, a difference exists between deep facts and observed data, but both must somehow be dealt with in an adequate theory of language and in any language teaching.

THE CONSEQUENCES FOR TEACHING

In order to decide what these facts mean for pedagogy, specifically for language teaching, it is necessary to look closely at some possible teaching strategies to assess their value. The first strategy might derive from finding translation equivalents. Students can be warned that the English structure in 4 has different meaning possibilities depending on the lexical items which are chosen to fill the structure, and then they can be required to translate a variety of sentences from and into English to reinforce this warning. Little more needs to be said about such a strategy, except to point out that all kinds of learning theories could be employed to teach the particular facts that are involved: stimulus-response or cognitive-code learning theories.

A second strategy would be one based on teaching students all the paraphrase relationships exemplified in sentences 11 to 13 so that they somehow intuitively come to an understanding of the differences in meaning that are involved in 1 to 3. Of course, such teaching would have to employ practice with adjectives other than those used in these examples. An optimal variety of such a strategy might require the presentation of diagrams such as those in 16 to 18 as an aid to learning. In one variety of this strategy teachers sometimes stress mastery of such mappings as 16 to 18 rather than of such sentences as 11 to 13 as a result of an overenthusiasm for the wrong things in linguistic theory, that is an enthusiasm for symbols and diagrams rather than for the understandings that linguists attempt to capture in these symbols and diagrams. This variation may even become a strategy of its own in second-language teaching. It has long been, and still continues to be, a major strategy in first-language teaching, where "knowing one's grammar" means knowing how to parse or diagram sentences.

A third strategy is to assume that students know certain things and that it is highly uneconomical to teach them what they already know. Sentences 19 and 20 can be used to illustrate this strategy:

19 Subduing lions can be dangerous.

20 Growling lions can be dangerous.

If a student knows the meaning of *subdue, growl,* and *lion,* he must understand *lions* to be the object of the verb *subduing* in 19 and to be the subject of the verb *growling* in 20, because sentences 21 and 22 are not possible in that they do not "make sense":

21 *Lions subdued someone.

22 *Someone growled lions.

Applying this same strategy to sentences 1 to 3, we can argue that since it does not make sense to say sentences like 23 to 26, we need not involve ourselves with this distinction at all because students obviously will not want to talk nonsense:

23   *The boy is easy to please John.
24   *The lesson is eager to please.
25   *The lesson is easy to please.
26   *The lesson is certain to understand.

However, there are serious doubts that this particular strategy is viable: it is impossible to be sure what parts of a speaker's knowledge of his own language and of the world viewed through that language will carry over to the second language. Linguists currently say that every speaker knows a great deal about his language; however, this knowledge is extremely abstract and concerns such matters as the ready availability of formal linguistic devices, such as the cycling and crossover principles and a knowledge that he can talk about anything provided only that he has words for certain concepts. In other words, when we appeal to the learner to use his knowledge of the meanings of items such as *boy, easy, eager, certain*, and *please* to decide what is sensible and what is not, we tend to beg the question of what exactly is involved in the language-learning process rather than provide an answer.

A fourth strategy might be one which calls for an ordered presentation of the structures, if such an ordering can be provided. The particular order chosen quite often derives from a theory of language, from what that theory holds must be explained in language, and from the form the explanation must take. In Krohn's revision of *English Sentence Patterns, English Sentence Structure* (1971), the author adopts the strategy of teaching the pattern *The boy is eager to please* first, because *the boy* is the subject of both *eager* and *please*. However, only a little practice is given. Then the structure *The boy is easy to please* is introduced and practiced while the student's attention is drawn to the fact that it contrasts in subtle ways with the first structure. Specifically, the student is to become aware that *the boy* is the grammatical subject of *easy* and the deep object of *please* in this pattern. The structure with *certain* is ignored in the revision on the grounds that it is impossible to teach everything, and there seems to be no reason to teach the structure with *certain* just because the linguist knows it exists.

A fifth strategy is exemplified in William Rutherford's *Modern English* (1968). This strategy requires students to develop the ability to handle various structures by means of ingenious exercises labeled *transformation*, *integration*, and *free reply*, which require students to have a tremendous amount of linguistic sophistication in English. Many of the exercises perhaps even require that students already possess the very sophistication they claim to be teaching.

A sixth strategy might entail the teaching of sets of paraphrases such as those in 11 to 13. The students' attention can be drawn to sentences such as 23 to 26 which are ungrammatical and their understanding of English can be tested by presenting sentences like 27 to 30 and requiring them to be classified as grammatical or not:

27   *The book is polite to go.

28   *The lesson is anxious to study.

29   The task is difficult to do.

30   The girl is nice to know.

Finally, the students could be allowed to judge their own and each other's novel creations for acceptability.

Various assumptions have been made about certain psychological factors in this discussion of possible teaching strategies. It would be well to make these assumptions explicit at this point. The first is that a certain amount of explanation is necessary in second-language teaching: the approach cannot be entirely *inductive*. However, it cannot be entirely *deductive* either, and it certainly should not overemphasize the use of diagrams such as 16 to 18. We must also assume we are dealing with rational individuals when we teach a second language, beings who behave in very systematic ways and exemplify controlled behavior, undoubtedly not always controlled in the way we want it but controlled nevertheless. The problem in teaching is to develop the controls we want in learners who are essentially rational. A third assumption is that language is used to express meanings and that students want to indulge in meaningful language exercises. It may well be argued that drill is meaningful. However, most students do not willingly accept the argument, no more than they accept arguments for doing hours and hours of finger exercises in order to learn to play the piano. A fourth assumption is that second-language learning is hard work and that most of this work has to do with learning a lot of completely arbitrary things to make them habitual: sounds, words, structures, and so on. Even Rutherford (1968) acknowledges this fact in his generative-transformationally-oriented text by providing great quantities of drill. One of the major tasks in developing a second-language-teaching methodology is to strike a proper balance between the need to use language meaningfully for communication and the need to learn the arbitrary characteristics which make that communication possible.

CONCLUSION

Several conclusions seem warranted. The first is that more is being discovered about English syntax every day; however, we are still a very long way from knowing a great deal about it. Even the information that appears in the latest books and articles may be best described as tentative in nature; in fact tentativeness is one of the most interesting characteristics of the rhetoric of current linguistics.

The second is that two different kinds of things must be acquired in learning any language, first or second: one is the actual forms the speakers of the language use and the other is the meanings of these forms. Current linguistics provides us with insights into how the two are related, and it compels us to assume that this relationship is important and must be taught. Such sentences as 1 to 3 force us to make a deep-surface distinction which we must then provide for all sentences in the language. The crucial problem is how to make use of these insights in devising teaching strategies.

The third conclusion is that languages have to be learned and that teachers can provide only so much help in the learning process. How can we teach English as a second language when we know so little about language in general, about any one language in particular, and about language learning itself? This point is emphasized because for a long time the focus has been on language teaching rather than on language learning. We must be prepared to present data to our students, but not random data, in the hope that they achieve insights into the structure of the language and at the same time acquire the ability to use the language. Since generative-transformational grammar provides us with the best insights that are available, we must make use of these in our teaching. It is ensuring that our students acquire these same insights that creates the difficulty. They must acquire these insights and they must learn to handle the surface patterns. We must assume too that the surface patterns themselves are very important.

Language structure, both deep and surface, is important in our teaching. A second language itself must be taught in a meaningful way if it is to serve the communicative needs of our students. Linguistic findings are important for the insights they give to teachers into meaning, into language patterning, and into the overall communicative process. Linguistic findings are not things to be taught directly though, because they are highly artifactual, or theory-biased, and they cover only one part of what must be learned. Linguistic findings themselves tell us almost nothing at all about how that one part should be taught or learned. Second-language teaching involves much more than presenting a set of linguistic structures colored by one linguistic theory or another in a way which is intuitively satisfying to the teacher.

In spite of a long history of second-language teaching, we have ventured only a little way in understanding what that history really means and in predicting what the future will hold for language teachers. Certainly, current views of language structure should influence teaching, but radical changes in views of such structure should not cause paralysis or a crisis of confidence. It is time to stress some of the other aspects of language teaching: time to look at the psychology and sociology of language learning; time to consider the total context of communication; and time to devise a pedagogy based on solid experimentation rather than on intuition. In such a broad context, language structure would be only one factor in language teaching and learning, and a commitment to a consideration of all the factors would give us some of the stability we need in a time of great change in linguistics.

chapter fourteen
Teaching Phonology

One fundamental assumption behind much of what is done in classrooms in second-language instruction is that language lives in the throat and mouth and not on paper, that is that language is essentially speech. Consequently, in the linguistic literature appear such statements as "language is speech not writing"; "the spoken language is 'primary' and the written language is 'secondary'"; "all human beings have access to systems of sounds, whereas many have no access to writing systems to represent these systems of sounds"; and "children always learn to speak before they learn to write." Although most linguists would agree on the validity of these statements about language, it is not so clear that they have direct relevance to formulating a methodology for language teaching. Such a methodology must draw heavily on linguistic knowledge, but methods and techniques employed by linguists for doing research in linguistics are not necessarily appropriate for teachers engaged in the task of teaching foreign languages. Too often in the past methods and techniques from the former area were extrapolated into the latter area, sometimes successfully to be sure, but the result has inevitably been a very constricting total approach to language teaching.

A VIEW OF LANGUAGE

There is however, total agreement among linguists that all languages are systematic and that the sounds of languages are systematic too. If a person must learn the sound system of English in order to speak English, we must be fairly sure what that system is like when we presume to teach it. An examination of textbooks designed to teach English to non-English speakers published in recent years conveys the impression that the sound system of English is generally well understood and that ways of teaching it have been rather well worked out. For example, the sound system is said to consist of a set of functional contrastive units called phonemes. This set of phonemes is small and finite, even though there is apparently more than a little disagreement as to the exact number of units in the set depending on whose system one chooses: for example, that of Fries and Pike or that of Trager and Smith. Basically though, there is agreement that words such as *beat*, *bit*, *bait*, *bet*, and *bat* contrast in their vowel phonemes. Since native speakers of English make these contrasts quite automatically, one major task which confronts a student who is learning English as a second language is mastery of this contrastive system of sounds.

Quite often the sound system, or the phonology, of a language has been described as though it existed completely independently of the syntactic system. Indeed for a long time many linguists decreed that it was absolutely necessary to maintain a strict separation between the phonological and syntactic systems of a language. These systems were regarded as completely independent of each other because of the so called "duality" feature in language design: that is each language has two independent subsystems, one of sounds and the other of meanings. Moreover, there was considerable insistence that the details of the phonology should be worked out without recourse to syntactic information so as to avoid the error of "level-mixing." It is possible today to observe some of the consequences of this view of phonology in certain current practices. For example, it leads to, and may seem to justify, a separation of phonetic drills from meaningful practice with the language in exercises which require students to discriminate among sounds and to mimic sounds, without requiring them to associate these sounds with any particular meanings or syntactic functions. This view of an autonomous phonology may even seem to justify the use of nonsense syllables and nonsense expressions in teaching, together with an injunction to students to be less concerned about what something means than about what it sounds like.

There are two other dichotomies which considerably influence how the phonology of English is taught to non-native speakers of English. Not only does there tend to be a more or less rigid separation of the teaching of phonology from the teaching of syntax, but there is a similar strict separation between teaching speaking skills and writing skills, and, within skills teaching, a separation between teaching what may be called the receptive skills and the productive skills. The dichotomy between speech and writing arises from the fact that writing is a representation of speech and that in first-language learning the acquisition of the spoken language always precedes that of the written language. Consequently, in second-language teaching and learning an emphasis has been placed on teaching the skills used in listening and speaking before those used in reading and writing. Students, no matter how literate they may be, are required to master the spoken forms of language before they see the language in print lest they misunderstand their language-learning task or suffer interference from the apparently unphonetic spelling system of English or from a carry-over of reading habits from the first language. The second dichotomy, the listening-speaking one, is founded on a belief that receptive skills are basic to productive ones. For example, it is assumed that until a learner can hear the difference between *beat* and *bit,* or until he can distinguish a statement intonation from a question intonation when the basic sentence structure is the same, as in *Your're ready* and *You're ready?*, it is impossible for him to produce the differences.

Although it is possible to question the validity of all three of the aforementioned dichotomies, they can appear to be very soundly based, for it is possible to present a more or less plausible case for the separation of phonology from syntax, of speaking from writing, and of receptive from productive skills, offering arguments ostensibly based on the nature of language and the nature of learning. For many years linguists and language teachers did present such a case. However, if the views of the nature of language and language learning on which the dichotomies are based are somewhat suspect, as they are at present, the dichotomies may be suspect too, and teaching methods based on them may well need to be reexamined. It may not be necessary to abandon the teaching methods, but the possibility does exist that a greater variety of instructional methods may become available if the dichotomies are abandoned, with a consequent increase in the effectiveness of instruction.

SOME PRACTICES

At this point it would be appropriate to examine some of the practices that are used in the classroom to teach phonology. First of all, drill work on minimal contrasts in the target language is widely used so that students learn to differentiate the odd word in such sets as *beat-beat-bit* and *mate-met-mate.* Then, students learn to pronounce the word which contains what can be called the "new" sound. This sound may be new in one of two different ways. The sound may exist in the first language as an allophonic variant of a phoneme, just as the Spanish [ð] exists as a variant of the Spanish /d/ phoneme. In this case the student learning English must learn to distinguish English *den* and *then*, and *ladder* and *lather*, and then to produce the different English words. In effect he must make himself conscious of a distinction which he made unconsciously before, that is, a distinction between the sounds [ð] and [d] and at the same time he must learn to make the distinction in a variety of positions in English: for example, initially, medially, and finally in words.

In other cases the actual sound is quite new to the learner and must be mastered in some other way. The second problem then is one of teaching or learning entirely new sounds in order to combat still another kind of interference from the first language. A variety of approaches can be used. Students may be asked to exercise the ability to mimic strange sounds. Such ability is sometimes said to decrease with age, children being better able to mimic than adults. Then, again, the ability apparently varies with individuals independently of age, because some people are much better or much worse at mimicry than the average. The mimicry practice can be done in various ways: for example, students may be asked to speak their first language with a target-language accent, or to try to mimic utterances. Anyone who is familiar with audiolingual teaching techniques knows that considerable emphasis is placed on exercises designed to improve students' ability to mimic utterances in the target language.

In order to combat possible interference from the first language much stress is placed on pronunciation practice on those features from the first language which carry over to the target language and also on those features of the target language which, being entirely new, must be controlled so as not to impede communication. Consequently, there is an emphasis on specifics: for example, on a subset of the total set of consonants, vowels, and distributional patterns of the target language. Within this subset there is a concentration of emphasis on eliminating carry-over from the first language to the target language, on making allophonic distinctions, and on altering distributional patterns. However, carry-over from the first language to the target language is encouraged for the remaining part of the total set. Such an emphasis is justified on the basis that it is necessary to teach the problems only and that some carry-over will always occur from the first to the second language. Some of this carry-over will obviously be an obstacle to the learner, but, depending on the two languages involved, a lot of it will turn out to be most helpful.

Often the actual teaching is done in such a way that much attention must be given to the choice of a notation system for the phonetic distinctions to be mastered. Students are therefore often required to master a vocabulary of phonetic terms. In some variations of the audiolingual approach much time, particularly at the beginning of the course, is spent on teaching phonetics. Students are asked to acquire some sophistication in talking about the distinctions they are being taught and about the articulatory nature of these distinctions, and considerable time may be spent in actually reading phonetic notation. Students are treated almost as though they were students of linguistics, not students of a foreign language.

In all of this work the goal of the teacher is one of helping his students acquire the ability to speak the target language intelligibly. Consequently, the pace of the utterances being taught is kept near that of native speakers of the target language; all the major phonemic distinctions are taught; control of the suprasegmental characteristics of stress, pitch, and pause is practiced; and students are given massive amounts of drill in both classroom and language laboratory to establish the new habits of the target language.

SOME RESTRICTIONS

This approach to teaching English phonology is very constrictive in the range of methods it allows teachers to employ. In order to show this, though, it is necessary to point out several of the shortcomings of the methods outlined above. For example, the assumption that language is speech not writing, while valid as a statement about *language*, is not valid as a guiding principle in *language teaching* when students are already literate. No literate person ever considers language to be only speech; it is certainly much more, and teachers would be unwise to ignore that fact.

Secondly, the view of the sound system itself that is incorporated in teaching and the notion that phonological facts may be separated from syntactic and semantic ones currently finds little support among linguists. This second objection is particularly strong in view of the fact that teachers using the audiolingual method have insisted that one of its great pillars of strength is its linguistic basis. Today the very soundness of the linguistics on which the method is apparently based is called into question. The current position is that the linguistic knowledge incorporated into most audiolingual courses is far from the best linguistic knowledge now available.

Thirdly, the various dichotomies mentioned earlier—between

phonology and syntax, between speech and writing, and between receptive and productive skills—can be maintained only at a considerable cost. Phonology and syntax appear today to be inseparably fused and not to be discrete levels of linguistic organization. Today, too, syntax seems to be more important than phonology in that it is somehow more central in an overall description of a language; therefore, one could argue that it should receive more emphasis at first. Similarly, speech and writing are closely connected both in the literate learner and in the fact that the writing systems of such languages as English and French can be shown to be rather good representations of phonological information. And, finally, both psychological and linguistic evidence exists to suggest that there is both an articulatory and a syntactic basis to the perception of phonological information.

It is also useful to contrast the view of phonology usually found in the audiolingual method with the one put forward in recent years by the generative-transformationalists. A major claim of the generative-transformationalists is that phonology is an integral part of a total language system, not one of several discrete and independent levels: phonology, morphology, syntax—and perhaps semantics. They postulate abstract phonological entities called *systematic phonemes* and a set of rules which operate to realize these systematic phonemes in sound, that is as some kind of phonetic substance. This set of rules is universally constrained in various interesting ways and the entities the rules operate on, the systematic phonemes, are optimal in the sense that they preserve very important relationships among words such as *sane* and *sanity*, *sign* and *signal*, *permit* and *permission*, and *mode* and *modify*, to cite but a few examples.

The theory claims that a speaker of English has acquired certain phonological knowledge as a result of speaking the language. Some of this knowledge that Chomsky and Halle ascribe to the speaker in the *The Sound Pattern of English* (1968) is of great interest. The native speaker of English evidently has no phonemic schwa vowel, only a phonetic one, so that [ə] is always a reduced full vowel. He also assigns stress phonetically not phonemically, there being only basically stressed and unstressed vowels with this difference quite predictable. He also has an underlying set of systematic phonemes which is rather well represented by current English orthography, particularly if he is a literate educated adult.

SOME NEW APPROACHES

The particular problem that is of interest today is how to build the knowledge of English phonology that native speakers have, as that knowledge is currently understood, into someone learning English as a second language, particularly someone who is literate and who has a need to use the language in both its spoken *and* written forms. It is a common experience in using the audiolingual approach with literate adults that even beginning students want to write down what they are learning. A completely audiolingual approach does not work very successfully for more than a few days if paper and pencils are banished from the classroom and serious problems of morale sometimes occur. Of course, such a fact may be more indicative of the way students have been previously conditioned to learn than of an inherent inadequacy in the approach we use. Such conditioning has a powerful effect on human beings and plays an important part in the need to reach for paper and pencils. However, other psychological factors come into operation too. Language is speech and no more than speech only for the *non*literate: for the literate, language is both speech and writing. Moreover, English orthography is not as bad as people like George Bernard Shaw have made it out to be with such spellings as *ghoti* for *fish*. It was certainly not bad for the taxonomic linguist, who went from sound to spelling in his phoneme-grapheme correspondences, and it is a whole lot better again for the generative-transformationalist. English spelling could be a good crutch for learners and one that should be used in certain circumstances.

Then, again, the sounds of a language do not exist apart from the meanings that the language conveys. Admittedly, sounds can be discussed independently of meanings but really only in the sense that magnetic tapes, phonograph records, parrots, and mimics deal with sounds, or certain structural linguists do for artifactual reasons. Indeed, the claim that sounds and meanings in every language are intimately fused may be stated even more strongly as follows: It is surely false to suppose that in the perception of speech one works out what sounds one has heard in an utterance and then, and only then, tries to put these sounds into some kind of syntactic and semantic framework, that is that one uses some kind of consecutive processing, first of all working out what sounds one has heard and then figuring out a meaning for them. Any processing that is involved is surely concurrent: a processing of sounds, syntax, and semantics together, with almost certainly the first strongly controlled by the second and third. Likewise, in speaking, all three dimensions are involved at once. No more than a very weak case can be made for teaching phonology as a part of language which is somehow separate from syntax and semantics. Note that the separation of syntax, phonology, and semantics in a generative-transformational grammar is acknowledged to be an artifact of presentation, not one of theory as it was in structural grammar. Chomsky himself has strongly insisted on this point in some of his work.

Given these circumstance—namely, a new description of English phonology which makes the claims it does, a sympathetic attitude toward the English spelling system, literate adult learners, and established learning patterns—we are forced to ask ourselves how we can construct an optimal system for teaching English, particularly English phonology in this instance. This approach involves basic acceptance of the general claims advanced by Chomsky and Halle in *The Sound Pattern of English* (1968), for their paradigm seems to be the most fruitful one within which to work in current linguistics. It is not necessary, however, to accept all the details of that treatment. We should note, too, the importance of recognizing the age and type of learner involved: in this case *adult, literate,* and *educated.* Given a different kind of learner, a five-year-old nonliterate, entirely different strategies would be called for. Perhaps one of the greatest weaknesses of the audiolingual method has been that it has tended to treat the literate, educated adult, as though he were a five-year-old child! He is not, and cannot be, and we must recognize that fact.

The problem then is one of putting all our knowledge of the language and of our students to work most efficiently with the goal the mastery of the phonology of English. We must work out a system whereby from the first we can present our students with the sounds of English and the spellings of English *concurrently.* We have tended in the past to concentrate on developing a metalanguage of phonetic symbols and terminology in the hope that we can help students master the traditional phonemic system. At some later state, generally unspecified, the students were expected to become literate in English through recognizing patterns of phoneme-grapheme correspondences if they had enough will-power: "literacy-by-osmosis" would be a suitable name for the process involved. Certainly that is how literacy seems to be achieved—if it is ever achieved within the audiolingual method! The suggestion made here is that we use not a purely phonetic metalanguage but rather one which combines certain basic terms from phonetics with regular alphabetic symbols. It is probably just as easy for students to use the regular alphabet in classes in English phonology as it is for them to learn a phonetic alphabet, even if they are literate in a Romance language. There are certainly no more difficulties in the task. If students are going to confuse statements about sounds with statements about letters, they can do it just as easily with a phonetic alphabet as they can with the regular English alphabet. The regular orthography has the additional advantage for a learner that he can relate sounds to letters in meaningful words which he can find written in exactly that way all around him. In effect, the use of the regular orthography eliminates a stage of learning for the student, a stage which, in the experience of many, he often tries to avoid anyway.

Employing the regular orthography from the beginning has further advantages because the orthography has certain consistencies built into it which a phonetic or phonemic transcription does not have. For example, it relates morphemes which appear in different phonetic shapes in different words: *sign* and *signify*, *phone* and *phonic*, and *please* and *pleasant*. At first this might seem to be as much a disadvantage as an advantage, but disadvantage it is not. The different phonetic shapes of morphemes are usually systematic in their variation, since the suppletive process is very rare indeed in English, confined as it is to such items as *go-went*, *good-better*, and *am-is-was*. Often the variation that is involved is below the conscious awareness of native speakers, as in the formation of noun plurals in *-s*. It should be our task in teaching English to a non-native speaker of English to help him develop this same subconscious control. It is for this reason that we must arrange for different allomorphic variants to be presented to the learner systematically. There is no reason in the audiolingual approach for relating *sign* to *signal*, or *face* to *facial*, or *Spain* to *Spanish*, but there is every reason for doing so if language is to be taught as a functional whole. In the same way it is to be hoped that we can help the foreign student to master such phenomena as stress assignment, palatalization, tensing and laxing, and so on.

A few brief examples follow of the kinds of data that we should attempt to build into our teaching materials in the hope that we can concurrently develop in students *phonetic control* of the actual sounds speakers of English use—though not of course perfect phonetic control, for we are not training either parrots or spies—together with subconscious mastery of the *phonological system*. There is an important dual emphasis: phonetics and phonology.

We must attempt to teach minimal contrasts of the *bin-pin* kind whether these contrasts are shown in the orthography by single letters (*b*,*p*) or by diagraphs such as *th* as in *thin*. Contrasts such as *pin-pine* and *tub-tube* are likewise important because of the orthographic connection of the vowels with a mute final *e* and because of the derivational system of English. This mute *e* is likewise important in words like *flee*, *pie*, *doe*, and *blue* where it shows the tenseness of the underlying vowel. Other subtle kinds of phonological patterns are revealed in the spelling system as, for example, the palatalization of the *s*'s in *press-pressure*, or the *c* in *face-facial*, or the neutralization of stressed vowels before *r* as in *fern*, *girl*, and *turn*. There are certain systematic phonological processes at work in English words and the orthography captures many of these processes in systematic ways. Students should be taught both the phonetic realizations and the processes in a methodical way: that is they should be taught the phonetic forms that speakers use and the principles that speakers are apparently following in producing these forms. To teach one without the other would be unsatisfactory.

We can see the advantages of such an approach most clearly in connection with the teaching of English stress. The Trager-Smith system recognizes four degrees of stress, and stress assignment seems largely unpredictable: hence the four degrees are said to be phonemic. Students learning English as a second language are consequently faced with the task of learning the stress assignment patterns of words almost as one learns the meanings of new words, item by item. However, to a native speaker of English stress assignment in words is fairly predictable. If stress is entirely or almost entirely predictable for a native speaker of English, we must instill in the learner of English as a second language those same intuitions about stress, or at least as many of them as we can. These intuitions may well be acquired if we systematically arrange work on pronunciation to show how stress is assigned in words such as *ángle*, *eléct*, *góssip*, *defér*, *cáptain*, *ágony*, *ánecdote*, *archáic*, and so on. There are many words which exhibit exactly the same stress characteristics as these, and such patterns seem to be as important to the student who is to communicate effectively in English as mastery of the *beat-bit* distinction, unless we expect him to talk in monosyllables all his life. Likewise, shifting of the kind we observe in *pólitics*, *political*, and *politícian* is also important.

CONCLUSION

It is safe to conclude these comments on present methods of teaching English phonology by pointing out that much of what we do is necessary. Students must develop phonetic control of the language, and many of the methods we employ in the classroom to help them to acquire such control. But we should note the deliberate use of the words *necessary* and *phonetic*. The word *necessary* is not used in conjunction with its familiar partner *sufficient*. What we do is necessary but hardly sufficient because our goal must be more than the phonetic one. It must be mastery of the phonology of English, so that students develop intuitions about the sound system of English in addition to the phonetic abilities achieved by mimics and parrots. Recent work in generative-transformational theory which focuses on English phonology holds great promise to teachers of English as a foreign language. It promises to help us to organize a lot of data which have been with us for many years, as, for example, the data in Wijk's *Rules of Pronunciation for the English Language* (1966) and in Marchand's *The Categories and Types of Present-Day English Word Formation* (1969). The next major development in teaching English phonology to non-English speakers will probably be in this area, but unfortunately as yet almost nothing exists that is of use in our classrooms.

part five

Linguistics and Contrastive Analysis

chapter fifteen
Contrastive Analysis

Students of linguistics encounter a number of very interesting hypotheses concerning different aspects of language and language function. One long-lived hypothesis which has attracted considerable attention from time to time—but more, it must be added, from psychologists and anthropologists than from linguists—is the Sapir-Whorf hypothesis with its claim that the structure of a language subtly influences the cognitive processes of the speakers of that language.

A more recent hypothesis, and one much more intriguing to linguists today than the Sapir-Whorf hypothesis, is the language-acquisition-device hypothesis proposed by the generative-transformationalists. This hypothesis is that infants are innately endowed with the ability to acquire a natural language and all they need to set the process of language acquisition going are natural language data. Only by postulating such a language-acquisition device can a generative-transformationalist account for certain linguistic universals, including, of course, not only one very important universal, the ability to learn a first language with ease, but also, apparently, another universal, the inability to learn a second language after childhood without difficulty. Like the Sapir-Whorf hypothesis, the language-acquisition-device hypothesis is extremely intriguing, but it too presents seemingly insurmountable difficulties to anyone seeking to devise a critical test of its truth or falsity. A linguist may accept the hypotheses because they usefully and economically explain certain language data that he seeks to account for according to a set of axioms he can accept; or he may reject the hypotheses because they appear to be mentalistic or subjective, or because he prefers a different set of axioms as the basis for his work.

Still a third hypothesis is the contrastive-analysis hypothesis, a hypothesis of particular interest to those linguists who are engaged in language teaching and in writing language-teaching materials. However, the contrastive-analysis hypothesis also raises many difficulties in practice, so many in fact that it is tempting to ask whether it is really possible to make contrastive analyses. And, even if the answer to that question is a more or less hesitant affirmative, then one may well question the value to teachers and curriculum workers of the results of such analyses.

THE STRONG CONTRASTIVE-ANALYSIS HYPOTHESIS

The contrastive analysis hypothesis may be stated in two versions, a strong version and a weak version. The strong version seems quite unrealistic and impracticable, even though it is the one on which those who write contrastive analyses usually claim to base their work. On the other hand, the weak version does have certain possibilities for usefulness even though it is suspect in some linguistic circles.

It is possible to quote several representative statements of the strong version of the contrastive-analysis hypothesis. First of all, Lado in the preface to *Linguistics Across Cultures* (1957) writes as follows:

> The plan of the book rests on the assumption that we can predict and describe the patterns that will cause difficulty in learning, and those that will not cause difficulty, by comparing systematically the language and culture to be learned with the native language and culture of the student (p. vii).

Since Lado cites Fries in support of this proposition, an appropriate quotation from Fries' *Teaching and Learning English as a Foreign Language* (1945) would be the following one:

> The most efficient materials are those that are based upon a scientific description of the language to be learned, carefully compared with a parallel description of the native language of the learner (p. 9).

More recently, in Valdman's *Trends in Language Teaching* (1966), Banathy, Trager, and Waddle (1966) state the strong version as follows:

> ... the change that has to take place in the language behavior of a foreign language student can be equated with the differences between the structure of the student's native language and culture and that of the target language and culture. The task of the linguist, the cultural anthropologist, and the sociologist is to identify these differences. The task of the writer of a foreign language teaching program is to develop materials which will be based on a statement of these differences; the task of the foreign language teacher is to be aware of these differences and to be prepared to teach them; the task of the student is to learn them (p. 37).

The same idea is presented in each of these three statements, the idea that it is possible to contrast the system of one language—the grammar, phonology, and lexicon—with the system of a second language in order to *predict* those difficulties which a speaker of the second language will have in learning the first language and to construct teaching materials to help him learn that language.

An evaluation of this strong version of the contrastive-analysis hypothesis suggests that it makes demands of linguistic theory, and, therefore, of the linguist, that he is in no position to meet. At the very least this version demands of the linguist that he have available a set of linguistic universals formulated within a comprehensive linguistic theory which deals adequately with syntax, semantics, and phonology. Furthermore, it requires a theory of contrastive linguistics into which complete linguistic descriptions of the two languages being contrasted can be plugged so as to produce the correct set of contrasts between the two languages. Ideally, the linguist should not have to refer at all to speakers of the two languages under contrast for either confirmation or disconfirmation of the set of contrasts generated by any such theory of contrastive linguistics. He should actually be able to carry out his contrastive studies quite far removed from speakers of the two languages, possibly without even knowing anything about the two languages in question except what is recorded in the grammars being used. Such seems to be the procedure which the strong version of the contrastive-analysis hypothesis demands. Stated in this way, the strong version doubtless sounds quite unrealistic, but it should be emphasized that most writers of contrastive analyses try to create the impression that this is the version of the hypothesis on which they have based their work—or at least could base their work if absolutely necessary. Perhaps this is yet another instance of a "pseudo-procedure" in linguistics, a pseudo-procedure being a procedure which linguists claim they could follow in order to achieve definitive results if only there were enough time.

One variant of the strong version may be illustrated as follows for making comparisons between the phonological systems of two languages A and B. In this variant the linguist must possess statements concerning the phonemic systems of A and B together with statements about the positional variants of the phonemes. He need not necessarily subscribe to any belief in the phoneme as a fact rather than as a fiction or as a bundle of distinctive features rather than as a contrastive reference point. His only need is for descriptive statements of the two systems which provide him with complete coverage of the phonological data of the two languages, these statements made according to the same principles. In addition, the linguist requires that the significant units in the two systems be symbolized by drawing consistently from an inventory of symbols so that a "bilabial stop" in a language is symbolized as either /p/ or /b/ but never as /d/ , and a "high front vowel" is symbolized as /i/, /ɪ/, or /iy/ but never as /a/. In each case it is apparent that the symbol is as vague, or as precise, as the term which prompted it, that is /b/ is no more precise a designation than "voiced bilabial stop," and the only merit of the symbol over the term is its convenience. Finally, it is assumed that any utterance in a language can be described as a sequence of phonemes: "voiced bilabial stop followed by a high front vowel," or /bi/, and that such a description exhausts the data.

The simplest use of such systems requires statements of relationships between the two languages in terms of the presence of absence of phonemes in a diasystem. It results in such statements as Language A has /a/ and Language B has the "same" /a/, or that while Language A has /a/ Language B does not. It results too in the parallel listing of phonemic systems somewhat as follows:

Language A	Language B
/a/	/a/
/b/	/b/
/c/	- - -
/d/	- - -
/e/	/e/
/f/	/f/
——	/g/
——	/h/

Although such statements and contrasts are often made, there is no linguistic justification for them. There is no basis in linguistic theory for talking about the phoneme /a/ in a language-free context and the only basis for assuming that /a/$_A$ is the "same" or is "similar" to /a/$_B$ is a phonetic one or a behavioral one dependent on interlingual identification. This particular variant of the strong version is naive and unrevealing at the best and totally misleading at the worst. However, some refinements of this diasystemic approach which consider the phonetic characteristics of the phonemes, the ways the phonemes structure, and their distributions offer certain improvements.

A much more defensible variant of this version is one which is not diasystemic but is diaphonic. In this variation the positional variants, or allophones, of the phonemes are taken into account and contrasted rather than the phonemes themselves. Diasystemic contrasts tend to ignore allophonic variation and therefore actual sound substance except insofar as the choice of phonemic symbols in the diasystem is determined by underlying phonetic considerations. Diaphonic contrasts make use of positional variants and attempt to relate allphones in A to allophones in B rather than phonemes in A to phonemes in B directly. For example [a] an allophone of $/a/_A$ corresponds to [a] an allophone of $/a/_B$; hence $/a/_A$ and $/a/_B$ are in some sense the same and may be considered to have certain functional correspondences. Such diaphonic contrasts can be made as explicit and delicate, that is detailed, as seems necessary, and it is possible to list the characteristics of each allophone in considerable detail in order to classify various types of contrastive relationships. The following are some examples of possible relationships in a presentation which is intended to be suggestive rather than exhaustive:

		Language A		Language B	
1	/a/:	$x\begin{bmatrix}1\\2\\3\end{bmatrix}z$	—	$x\begin{bmatrix}1\\2\\3\end{bmatrix}z$	:/a/
2	/a/:	$x\begin{bmatrix}1\\2\\3\end{bmatrix}z$	—	$x\begin{bmatrix}1\\2\end{bmatrix}z$	:/a/
3	/a/:	$\left\{ x\begin{bmatrix}1\\2\\3\end{bmatrix}z \right.$	—	$x\begin{bmatrix}1\\2\end{bmatrix}z$	:/a/
		$\left. a\begin{bmatrix}3\\4\end{bmatrix}c \right.$	—	$a\begin{bmatrix}3\\4\end{bmatrix}c$	:/b/
4	/a/:	$\left\{ x\begin{bmatrix}1\\2\\3\end{bmatrix}z \right.$	—	$x\begin{bmatrix}1\\2\end{bmatrix}z$	:/a/
		$\left. a\begin{bmatrix}3\\4\end{bmatrix}c \right.$	—	$[?]c$	:"noise"
5	/a/:	$x\begin{bmatrix}1\\2\\3\end{bmatrix}z$	—	$x\begin{bmatrix}2\\3\\4\end{bmatrix}z$	
	/b/:	$x\begin{bmatrix}3\\4\end{bmatrix}z$	—	$x\begin{bmatrix}2\\3\\4\end{bmatrix}z$	:/a/

Another variant of this version uses either overlapping or side-by-side diagrams and charts employing phonetic norms for phonemes:

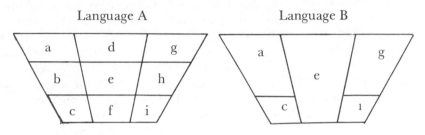

or density representations:

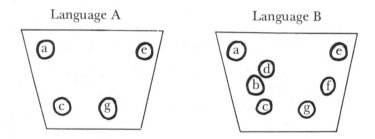

Diaphonic contrasts has considerable possibilities in its use of both systems and substance with the emphasis placed on the former. However, certain difficulties arise in practice, for complete diaphonic contrasts obviously require very complete descriptions of the systems being contrasted. But it is well known that in practice both completeness of description and uniqueness of description are unattainable goals. In addition, the problem is complicated by the necessary concern with two languages rather than one. More serious though is the fact that most systematic statements of the type referred to deal more or less, rather than completely, with higher level phonological patterning, syllable structure, stress distribution, neutralization, morpheme structure, and so on. It is impossible to make a rigorous contrast of the allophones of phonemes unless all the phonological details are known and not just certain highly frequent or easily observed ones.

Another problem relates to the classification of the contrasts between the two systems. Such terms as underdifferentiation and overdifferentiation, phone substitution, parallelism, and reinterpretation are used to classify the various possible cross-language relationships. In practice, the existing classifications do not work very well and considerable overlapping of classes results. Then, too, the overall contrast of the two systems leads to the prediction of relationships which are not in fact observed and to the nonprediction of relationships which are observed. Such predictive weaknesses apparently result from the use of either inadequate systems, inadequate classifications, or a mixture of both.

THE WEAK CONTRASTIVE-ANALYSIS HYPOTHESIS

In contrast to the demands made by the strong version, the weak version requires of the linguist only that he use the best linguistic knowledge available to him in order to account for observed difficulties in second-language learning. It does not require what the strong version requires, the prediction of those difficulties and, conversely, of those learning points which do not create any difficulties at all. The weak version leads to an approach which makes fewer demands of contrastive theory than does the strong version.

The weak version uses the evidence provided by interference as its starting point and works from such evidence toward relationships between systems rather than directly betwen systems. Linguistic systems are important, for there is no regression to a presystemic view of language nor is the result a mere classification of errors in any way that happens to be useful. The starting point in the contrast is provided by such evidence as phonological translation, interlingual indentification, perception of foreign accent, and so on, and the two systems are used only to explain the observed data of phonic interference. Consequently, there can be no unpredicted relationships and difficulties nor can there be non-occurring predicted relationships and difficulties because each statement concerning a relationship has an observed datum as its point of origin. An awareness of systems is important, however, to discourage over-analysis and to provide a basis for classifying and explaining the observed interference phenomena.

The simplest version of the approach is one that takes an utterance in Language A and accounts for how that utterance is heard by someone who speaks Language B. It assumes that the significant units, or emes, in A are materialized in etic substance, and that this substance is heard by a B listener who interprets it in the units of B, somewhat as follows:

Language A   Language B

emic units ———etic———— emic units
                     substance

The segments to be considered in this approach may be of any manageable size. In each case, however, in order to make a complete contrast it is necessary to specify everything that is present in a particular segment: stress, pitch, border phenomena, determined features, redundant features, and so on. No particular phonetic system is precluded from use in showing what is present in the etic substance of a particular segment; however, it is very likely that some phonetic systems may be more useful than others.

If the concern is with understanding how a B listener interprets an utterance in A, the model just given is appropriate. The utterance itself may be a single segment, as follows:

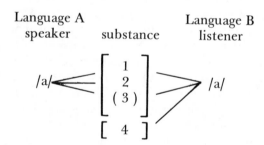

Language A   Language B
  speaker   substance   listener

In this example /a/$_A$ is produced in a particular environment with the three features [1], [2], and [(3)], the last of which is determined. B hears [1] and [3] but [2] escapes him and he supplies [4] himself so that he can interpret what he heard as [1], [3], and [4], or /a/$_B$. It may also be assumed from the symbolization that /a/$_A$ and /a/$_B$ are somehow similar in function in the two languages. Two further possibilities may be shown:

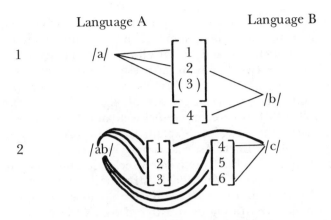

In the first of these /a/ ₐ is heard as /b/ ᵦ, that is as a different kind of contrast in B than in A; and in the second of these a cluster in A, in this case a two unit segment, is heard as a single unit segment in B.

Even more complicated types of analysis are both possible and desirable. The linguist has no reason for stopping with accounting for how a B listener hears an A utterance or particular segments in such an utterance. He can further inquire how the B listener then tries to pronounce that A utterance and how in turn the A speaker, now a listener, interprets that attempt:

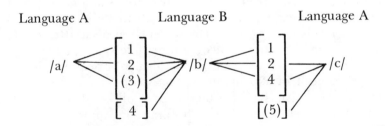

The weak version allows for very detailed contrasts based on actual interference phenomena, ranging from phonological translation at one extreme to residual foreign accent at the other. In every case a statement of contrast is anchored in evidence from sound substance, since such evidence alone necessitates that statement. Then, the particular contrast is classified into some kind of system. Since the approach recognizes the communicative process, this further reason would tend to recommend it over the strong version.

A close reading of most of the contrastive analyses which are available shows them to conform to some of the demands made by the weak version of the theory and not at all to the demands of the strong version. Even the two highly regarded texts on English and Spanish by Stockwell and Bowen, *The Sounds of English and Spanish* (1965) and *The Grammatical Structures of English and Spanish* (1965), fall into this category. Stockwell and Bowen appear to use their linguistic knowledge to explain what they know from experience to be problems English speakers have in learning Spanish. Their linguistic theory is actually extremely eclectic and contains insights from generative-transformational, structural, and paradigmatic grammars. Nowhere in the texts is there an obvious attempt to predict errors using an over-riding contrastive theory of any power. Even the hierarchy of difficulty which Stockwell and Bowen establish in the second chapter of the *Sounds* volume is based more on their experience and intuition than on an explicit theory for predicting difficulties.

SOME RECENT CLAIMS

In recent years two still different approaches have been taken to the problems of contrastive analysis, both resulting from the current enthusiasm for generative-transformational theory. One of these approaches dismisses the hypothesis from any consideration at all. This dismissal stems from a strong negative reaction to contrastive analysis, as, for example, in articles by Ritchie (1967) and Wolfe (1967) in *Language Learning*. The second approach attempts to use generative-transformational theory to provide some of the necessary over-riding theory to meet either the demands of prediction in the strong version or of explanation in the weak version.

The case for dismissal may be stated as follows: Languages do not differ from each other without limit in unpredictable ways, statements to the contrary notwithstanding. All natural languages have a great deal in common so that anyone who has learned one language already *knows* a great deal about any other language he must learn. Not only does he know a great deal about that other language even before he begins to learn it, but the deep structures of both languages are very much alike, so that the actual differences between the two languages are really quite superficial. However, to learn the second language, he must learn the precise way in which that second language relates the deep structures to its surface structures and their phonetic representations. Since this way is unique for each language, contrastive analysis can be of little or no help at all in the learning task because the rules to be internalized are unique. Even though the form and some of the content of the rules to be acquired might be identical for both languages, the combinations of these for individual languages are quite idiosyncratic so that superficial contrastive statements can in no way help the learner in his task.

The above argument has some merit. If the underlying vowel system of French is something like the one Schane outlines in *French Phonology and Morphology* (1968), and the underlying vowel system of English is something like the one Chomsky and Halle outline in *The Sound Pattern of English* (1968), and if the speaker of English must somehow internalize the underlying vowel system of French and the fifty or so phonetic realization rules which Schane gives in order to speak acceptable French, then one may easily be tempted to reject the whole notion of contrastive analysis, claiming that it has nothing at all to contribute to an understanding of the learning task that is involved.

Uncertainty is obviously piled upon uncertainty in making contrastive analyses. Such uncertainties arise from inadequacies in existing linguistic theories. As an example of theoretical inadequacy, one may observe that the notion of deep structure itself is extremely uncertain. N. Chomsky (1968), McCawley (1968), and Fillmore (1968) all mean different things by it, but all agree that it has something to do with meaning. However, for the purposes of contrastive analysis any claim that all languages are very much the same at the level of deep structure seems to be little more than a claim that it is possible to talk about the same things in all languages, which is surely not a very interesting claim, except perhaps in that it seems to contradict the one made by Sapir and Whorf. The preceding statement is not meant to be a criticism of generative-transformational theory; it is meant to show how acceptance of that theory can fairly easily lead one to reject the idea that it is possible to make contrastive analyses, or, put less strongly, to reject the idea that generative-transformational theory has something to contribute to a theory of contrastive analysis, given the present state of the art.

Many experienced teachers find themselves unable to accept such reasons for rejection of the hypothesis. Their experience tells them that a Frenchman is likely to pronounce English *thing* as *sink* and a Russian likely to pronounce it as *tink*, that a Spaniard will almost certainly fail to differentiate English *bit* from *beat*, and that an Englishman learning French will tend to pronounce the French word *plume* as *pleem* or *ploom*. They admit that in each case they must be prepared to teach the whole of the second language to a learner, but also insist that some parts of that second language are easier to learn than others, for no one ever must learn *everything* about the second language. However, many also admit that they do not know in what order learners should try to overcome the various difficulties they are observed to have. Should a Spaniard learning English learn to differentiate *bit* from *beat* and *bet* from *bait* because of the important surface contrasts which he does not make in Spanish? Or should he learn to associate the vowels in such pairs of words as *weep* and *wept, pale* and *pallid, type* and *typical, tone* and *tonic, deduce* and *deduction* so that he can somehow internalize the underlying phonological system of English?

Some recent suggestions for using generative-transformational theory in contrastive analysis have actually been attempts to bring powerful theoretical insights to bear within the weaker version of the hypothesis in order to explain observed interference phenomena, for example work by Ritchie (1968) and Carter (unpublished). In their work, Ritchie and Carter have used distinctive feature hierarchies in attempts to explain such problems as why a Russian is likely to say *tink* and a Frenchman *sink* for English *think*. Such work, using the notions of feature hierarchy, rule-cycling, and morpheme-structure and word-structure rules, has considerable possibilities. Certainly it seems more promising than other work which attempts to show gross similarities between deep structures in an assortment of languages.

CONCLUSION

In conclusion, it is fair to say that teachers of second or foreign languages are living in very uncertain times. A decade or so ago contrastive analysis was still a fairly new and exciting idea apparently holding great promise for teaching and curriculum construction. Now, one is not so sure—and not solely as a result of the Chomskyan revolution in linguistics. The contrastive-analysis hypothesis has not proved to be workable, at least not in the strong version in which it was originally expressed. This version can work only for one who is prepared to be quite naive in linguistic matters. In its weak version, however, it has proved to be helpful and undoubtedly will continue to be so, as linguistic theory develops. However, the hypothesis probably will have less influence on second-language teaching and on course construction in the next decade than it apparently has had in the last two decades.

part six

Linguistics and Language Variation

chapter sixteen
The Dialect Issue

Language varies in all kinds of ways: by time, place, age, sex, and social group to give but a few examples. We know that language changes over the centuries so that the English of Shakespeare must have sounded quite different from the English of today. We know too that Texans speak differently from Londoners and natives of Boston have quite different accents from those of Chicago. Children's speech is easily distinguished from that of adults, and often men and women choose different linguistic forms from each other. But the differences that seem to create the major problem to educators are those associated with social groups of one kind or another.

The schools have always attempted to teach something which has been called Standard English. However, it has never been easy to define exactly what Standard English is. It is not just simply the variety of the language assocated with educated speakers because regional accents make for more than one variety of pronunciation. Apparently, the standard is to be found less in pronunciation than in syntax and vocabulary. The syntax of users of Standard English tends to be much the same whether they are speaking or writing, though, of course, expression in each medium may at times suffer from the performance limitations brought about by the need to communicate on the spur of the moment. Schools have therefore tried to teach control of the syntax of formal written English to all students regardless of their social or regional background. Sometimes the task has been easy, as when students are already very familiar with the major characteristics of what is being taught. Sometimes the task has been very difficult, particularly when great differences have existed between the students' spoken dialect and the kind of English preferred by the school.

In recent years the problem has been compounded by large population movements from south to north and east to west, by criticisms that the schools are failing (although the critics often do

not agree on what would constitute success), and by increasing
pressures from minority social groups to gain recognition for what
they consider to be differences worth maintaining. At the center of
one of the resulting controversies is a phenomenon sometimes
referred to as Black English. It may be useful, therefore, to consider
some of the issues associated with this kind of English in an attempt
to understand their source, to evaluate various suggestions for dealing
with perceived related problems, and to determine what related
issues have been ignored. Black English is an emotion-laden topic
which seems to have generated more heat than light among those
who have attempted to deal with it.

BLACK ENGLISH

Certain linguists, particularly Stewart (1969) and Dillard (1972),
have proposed that a variety of English, which they call Black
English, is spoken by many black Americans in the social stratum in
which the head of the household is either a manual worker or is
unemployed. The majority of speakers are said to live in large
northern cities, often in ghettoes, and they or their families are often
recently removed from the south. There is no question that such
ghettoes exist and that such a migration has occurred. There is also
no question that the educational achievements of many black
children who live in northern ghettoes are minimal and are far behind
the achievements of white suburban children. What is not so clear is
that all these blacks, children and adults, speak something which can
be called Black English.

Linguists such as the two just mentioned and Labov (1970) and
Fasold and Wolfram (1970) have described some of the linguistic
characteristics they have found among black speakers. They have
observed that vowels are often nasalized and sometimes the
post-vocalic nasal is dropped so that *pin* can be [pĩn] or [pĩ]. Vowels
are also neutralized so that both *pin* and *pen* can be [pĩ]. Such
neutralization is particularly noticeable before *r* or *l*, which often
vocalize in addition. Final clusters often are simplified so that *test*
sounds like *Tess* and *mask* like *mass*. *Then* and *den* seem to be
interchangeable pronunciations of *then*, and *three* and *free* seem to
be interchangeable pronunciations of *three*. Final *-ing* comes out as
-in; in general unstressed initial syllables are lost: *'bout* and *'cept*;
and stress is often shifted forward: *Détroit, pólice,* and *hótel.* In
syntax the use of *do* is very different from the use of *do* in Standard
English, as in *I done baked a cake.* Likewise, the use, or non-use, of

be is different, as in *He be here soon* and *He here soon.* Agreement of subject and verb is also different: *He have done it* and *He walk there everyday;* multiple negation is very frequent; *ain't* abounds; and quite different statement forms are sometimes found: *I want to know did he do it* and *Didn't nobody see it.*

Such observations would appear to suggest that Black English is quite different from Standard English, in particular in having more homophones and some very different syntactic forms. Two key questions may be asked at this point: Is Black English homogeneous? Where did it come from? Finding answers to these questions is important if linguists and educators are to be able to offer constructive solutions to educational problems that cannot be ignored.

The homogeneity issue is perhaps the easier to deal with. There seems little reason to suppose that such homogeneity exises. The English spoken by black Americans seems to vary as widely as the English spoken by white Americans and there are no differences between the two for many black speakers. Yet it cannot be denied that many blacks do have certain speech characteristics which allow a listener, as on a telephone, to know that he is conversing with a black person rather than a white person. What is not clear is that this black person's English is almost exactly like another black person's English, that is that they both speak Black English. Descriptions of Black English make it sound much more homogeneous than it is. Of course, descriptions öf a standard variety of English would leave the same impression, for linguists tend to emphasize the systematic shared characteristics they find rather than those which tend to resist analysis because of their apparent randomness. There is considerable variety within Black English, a point which a careful investigator like Labov (1970) has made. The existence of such variety should lead to caution when solutions are proposed to pedagogical problems associated with teaching reading and language skills in ghetto schools.

The second problem concerns the historical reason for any differences that exist between Black English and other varieties, and that exact status of those differences today. Some scholars, for example Stewart (1967, 1968) and Dillard (1972), claim that Black English has quite a different source from many other varieties. They claim that it is not a form of British English transplanted to America which was learned by black slaves and then developed alongside varieties spoken by whites. It is not, therefore, a southern variety of American English. Rather, Black English is a creolized version of

English developing out of the slave trade and coming from the coasts of Africa and the Caribbean. Over the course of time it has gradually drifted toward Standard American English because of geographical and racial mixtures, but it still differs in certain fundamental ways.

This problem is important because if Black English has a historical development which is largely, or fundamentally, independent of that of other varieties of American English, then one can argue that some serious difficulties might result for speakers of Black English in having to speak or read Standard English. The differences are obviously not so great as those between English and French but it can be argued that by being more subtle, they are probably more formidable and persistent. The alternative view, which sees a common source for the varieties of English, would lead one to expect fewer problems and might encourage the adoption of quite different strategies.

These then are two controversial areas in discussions of Black English. The wisest course at the moment seems to be that which holds that while there is no homogeneous Black English many blacks do share to a greater or lesser extent certain speech characteristics and do vary considerably in the forms they use according to the occasion. Furthermore, it is not quite so apparent as it has been claimed that the empirical consequences of accepting one version of the history of Black English rather than another are so different. This point is particularly important when some of the pedagogical solutions are examined: it would not matter what kind of history Black English has had when some proposals are examined for they would be no more or no less workable with a quite different history.

LANGUAGE VARIATION

The most productive way of looking at dialect differences from the perspective of trying to understand how they operate in society is to regard them as functional varieties of language, each difference being associated with its own set of social variables. Language varies in all kinds of ways and groups use a particular language variety as one device for achieving, either consciously or subconsciously, group identification. People who work at the same tasks, live near each other, and associate together tend to speak alike, whereas different work tasks, residential preferences, and recreational pursuits tend to be associated with different speech characteristics. It is also pointless to say which causes which. But it is not pointless to observe that society as a whole prefers the characteristics associated with the "have's" to those associated with the "have-not's." Even though this is a social observation not a linguistic one, it cannot be ignored by any linguist who attempts to give educational advice.

We must recognize that language varies and probably that language differences cannot be eliminated. We must also recognize that it is very unlikely that people, and children in particular, will easily learn useless language skills. It is one thing to try to learn the skills required to function in the social context in which one finds himself; it is quite another thing to learn the skills one would require to function in a social context one *might* get an opportunity to function in one day. Actually it is difficult to see how one can learn the linguistic skills necessary to function in such a hypothetical situation, particularly when those skills are only a small fraction of the total set of skills that are necessary and the whole set must be acquired if the linguistic skills are to function properly. As Eliza Doolittle found, it is not enough to speak like a lady, one must also behave like a lady, and, still more important, be treated like a lady!

When dialect issues are fitted within the context of language variation and when, in addition, dialects are regarded not as homogeneous entitities but as linguistic abstractions, we see a need to recognize the importance of attaining an understanding of linguistic functions. How does a particular speaker use his linguistic skills in a certain setting? In different settings? What kinds of skills does he exhibit in listening? In speaking? In reading? In writing? How did he acquire these skills and how does he maintain them? These questions raise fundamental issues in connection not only with language function but also with language description and language acquisition. To deal adequately with them we need more comprehensive linguistic theories and descriptions than we currently have, and we need much more tentative solutions to problems we see than those currently proposed.

A body of theory is developing that should enable some progress to be made in understanding language variation. It exists in the writings of researchers such as Labov (1971), Hannerz (1969), Goffman (1971), Bernstein (1972), Lakoff (1970), and Hawkins (1969). Their work emphasizes such matters as the variability of language, the need to look at the contexts of language use, the functional differences of the "same" linguistic forms and the functional similarities of "different" linguistic forms, the different linguistic ecologies of social groups, and the role of language in the instructional process. Such work rather quickly reveals the inadequacies of most extant discussions of Black English in particular and dialects in general and the general bankruptcy of the pedagogical recommendations which linguists have made.

TWO PROPOSED SOLUTIONS

One proposal (Stewart, 1969; Dillard, 1972) for dealing with dialect differences has been to teach Standard English to speakers of nonstandard varieties of the language by methods used to teach English as a foreign language. This proposal assumes that it is desirable to make such speakers bidialectal and that a well-conceived pedagogy is available. It has been attacked as inadequate on both grounds.

Bidialectalism as a solution is basically unworkable because it flies in the face of what we should be aware of about language variation. A person becomes bidialectal if it is functionally useful to become bidialectal, perhaps as an actor, or as a traveler, or in order to move freely between social or regional settings which are very different from each other. But in a monodialectal setting, no functional value exists for bidialectalism, and in the absence of such reinforcement the only incentive to achieve bidialectism is the possibility of some kind of long-term reward for achievement of the goal. In actual fact becoming bidialectal is about as functional as learning Eskimo for many ghetto dwellers and even for many rural isolates. We need only look at the generally sorry state of foreign-language instruction to see what happens when language instruction has such remote ends! The ends of such instruction are remote for adolescents. How much more remote are the ends of bidialectalism for five-year olds! Bidialectalism as a goal is not attainable given the social setting in which we find ourselves. Those who advocate it are well-meaning but unrealistic. They should be criticized on this latter account rather than for hypocrisy, as unfortunately they have been by Sledd (1972).

The proposed means for attaining bidialectism by using methods for teaching English as a foreign language are also very inadequate. There is already considerable controversy about adequate ways for doing such teaching and no consensus exists as to what the best way is. But more important, there is every reason to suppose that bidialectalism and bilingualism are very different things insofar as they affect one's ability to communicate. Dialects are subtly different from each other whereas languages are grossly different; communication occurs across dialect differences but fails to across language differences. In general, it is easier to deal with gross differences which may be readily recognized than with subtle differences which are scarcely above the threshold of attention, particularly when these have many equally subtle social correlations.

Another proposal has been to develop some kind of transitional dialect readers so that beginning reading can be done in the nonstandard dialect of the child if he speaks such a dialect (Baratz and Shuy, 1969). However, there has been little acceptance of such readers by the public. This failure does not arise from the fact that the concept of dialect which the readers conform to may well be inadequate or that the readers may not be particularly good as readers. Rather, it arises from the fact that people do not accept readers written in dialect since they regard Standard English as the English of reading. And in a very real sense they are right! The language of reading is Standard English. Whether we like it or not that is a fact, and a rejection of that fact is likely to jeopardize any solution, no matter how well intentioned.

CONCLUSION

Dialect differences are a fact of life and of language. The linguist's task is to try to understand them and relate them to other relevant phenomena, many of which will be non-linguistic. Perhaps too much emphasis has been placed by linguists on the linguistic phenomena alone with a resulting overstatement of their conclusions.

One conclusion that has been overstated is that which recommends dialect change as a prerequisite to reading instruction. The case for acquiring a standard dialect in order to read English is not a strong one, particularly if English orthography is morphophonemic in nature. The advocacy of foreign-language teaching methodology is also an unjustified extrapolation. The dialect problem, if it is a problem, is largely a social one not a linguistic one. Linguists should exercise considerable caution in advocating their solutions to what they consider to be social ills. They might well have made completely inadequate diagnoses and they might end up by recommending operations which they consider will be successful but unfortunately kill the patient. Better diagnoses and more cautious prognoses are to be preferred to the kinds of remedies that are currently being proposed. Such remedies will come only if the consulting team is enlarged to include a much wider range of specialists than are involved at the moment.

Bibliography

Anthony, Edward M., "Approach, Method, and Technique," *English Language Teaching*, 17 (1963), 63-67.

Bailey, Mildred H., "The Utility of Phonic Generalizations in Grades One Through Six," *Reading Teacher*, 20 (1967), 413-18.

Banathy, Bela, Edith C. Trager, and Carl D. Waddle, "The Use of Contrastive Data in Foreign Language Course Development," in *Trends in Language Teaching*, Albert Valdman, ed. New York: McGraw-Hill, 1966.

Baratz, Joan C. and Roger W. Shuy, eds., *Teaching Black Children to Read*. Washington: Center for Applied Linguistics, 1969.

Barnhart, Clarence L., "A Reaction to Sister Mary Edward Dolan's Linguistics in Teaching Reading," *Reading Research Quarterly*, 2:3 (1967), 117-22.

Bernstein, Basil, "Social Class, Language and Socialization, in *Language and Social Context*, P.P. Giglioli, ed. Harmondsworth: Penguin Books, 1972.

Bever, Thomas G., J.A. Fodor, and W. Weksel, "Is Linguistics Empirical?," *Psychological Review*, 72 (1965a), 492-500.

Bever, Thomas G., J.A. Fodor, and W. Weksel, "On the Acquisition of Syntax: A Critique of 'Contextual Generalization'," *Psychological Review*, 72 (1965b), 467-82.

Bever, Thomas G., J.R. Mehler, and V.V. Valian, "Linguistic Capacity of Very Young Children," ERIC Document, ED 018-796, 1968.

Bloom, Lois, *Language Development: Form and Function in Emerging Grammars*. Cambridge: M. I. T. Press, 1970.

Bloom, Lois, "Why not Pivot Grammar?," *The Journal of Speech and Hearing Disorders*, 36:1 (1971), 40-50.

Bloomfield, Leonard, "Why a Linguistic Society?," *Language*, 1 (1925), 1-5.

Bloomfield, Leonard, *Language*. New York: Henry Holt and Company, 1933.

Bloomfield, Leonard and Clarence L. Barnhart, *Let's Read*. Detroit: Wayne State University Press, 1961.

Bloomfield, Leonard and Clarence L. Barnhart, *Let's Read, Part 1 (Experimental Edition)*. Bronxville: C. L. Barnhart, Inc., 1963.

Bond, G. L. and E. B. Wagner, *Teaching the Child to Read*. 3rd ed. New York: Macmillan, 1960.

Braine, Martin D. S., "On Learning the Grammatical Order of Words," *Psychological Review*, 70 (1963a), 323-48.

Braine, Martin D. S., "The Ontogeny of English Phrase Structure: The First Phase," *Language*, 39 (1963b), 1-13.

Braine, Martin D. S., "On the Basis of Phrase Structure: A Reply to Bever, Fodor, and Weksel," *Psychological Review*, 72 (1965), 483-92.

Brown, Roger, *Social Psychology*. New York: Free Press, 1965.

Brown, Roger and Ursula Bellugi, "Three Processes in the Child's Acquisition of Syntax," *Harvard Educational Review*, 34 (1964), 133-51.

Brown, Roger and Jean Berko, "Psycholinguistic Research Methods," in *Handbook of Research Methods in Child Development*, P. H. Mussen, ed. New York: Wiley, 1960.

Brown, Roger, Courtney B. Cazden, and Ursula Bellugi, "The Child's Grammar from 1 to 111," in *The 1967 Minnesota Symposium on Child Psychology*, J. P. Hill, ed. Minneapolis: University of Minnesota Press, 1968.

Bull, William E., *Spanish for Teachers: Applied Linguistics*. New York: Ronald Press, 1965.

Burmeister, Lou E., "Usefulness of Phonic Generalizations," *Reading Teacher*, 21 (1968), 349-56, 360.

Buswell, Guy T., "The Process of Reading," *Reading Teacher*, 13 (1959), 108-14.

Carroll, John B., "Language Development in Children," in *Encyclopedia of Educational Research*. New York: Macmillan, 1960.

Carroll, John B., "Psychology," *North East Conference on the Teaching of Foreign Languages, Reports of the Working Committees*, 1966a.

Carroll, John B. "The Contributions of Psychological Theory and Educational Research for the Teaching of Foreign Languages," in *Trends in Language Teaching*, Albert Valdman, ed. New York: McGraw-Hill, 1966b.

Carroll, John B., "Some Neglected Relationships in Reading and Language Learning," *Elementary English*, 43 (1966c), 577-82.

Carter, Richard J., "An Approach to a Theory of Phonetic Difficulties in Second-Language Learning." Bolt Beranek and Newman Inc., Report 1575.

Cazden, Courtney B., "Environmental Assistance to the Child's Acquisition of Grammar." Unpublished doctoral dissertation, Harvard University, 1965.

Center for Applied Linguistics, *Styles of Learning among American Indians: An Outline for Research*. Washington: Center for Applied Linguistics, 1969.

Chall, Jeanne, *Learning to Read: The Great Debate*. New York: McGraw-Hill, 1967.

Chomsky, Carol S., *The Acquisition of Syntax in Children from 5 to 10*. Cambridge: M. I. T. Press, 1969.

Chomsky, Carol S., "Reading, Writing, and Phonology," *Harvard Educational Review*, 40 (1970), 287-309.

Chomsky, Noam, *Syntactic Structures*. The Hague: Mouton, 1957.

Chomsky, Noam, "Review of B. F. Skinner's *Verbal Behavior*," *Language*, 35 (1959), 26-58.

Chomsky, Noam, "Comments for Project Literacy Meeting," *Project Literacy Reports*, 2 (1964), 1-8.

Chomsky, Noam, *Aspects of the Theory of Syntax*. Cambridge: M. I. T. Press, 1965.

Chomsky, Noam, "Linguistic Theory," *North East Conference on the Teaching of Foreign Languages, Reports of the Working Committees*, 1966.

Chomsky, Noam, *Language and Mind*. New York: Harcourt, Brace and World, 1968.

Chomsky, Noam and Morris Halle, *The Sound Pattern of English*. New York: Harper & Row, 1968.

Clymer, Theodore, "The Utility of Phonic Generalizations in the Primary Grades," *Reading Teacher*, 16 (1963), 252-58.

Coleman, Algernon, *The Teaching of Modern Foreign Languages in the United States*. New York: American and Canadian Committee on Modern Languages, 1929.

Cordts, Ann D., *Phonics for the Reading Teacher*. New York: Holt, Rinehart and Winston, 1965.

Cromer, R., "The Development of Temporal References During the Acquisition of Language." Unpublished doctoral dissertation, Harvard University, 1968.

Davis, David C., "Phonemic Structural Approach to Initial Reading Instruction," *Elementary English*, 41 (1964), 218-23.

Diack, Hunter, *The Teaching of Reading, in Spite of the Alphabet*. New York: Philosophical Library, 1965.

Dillard, Joey Lee, *Black English: Its History and Usage in the United States.* New York: Random House, 1972.

Diller, Karl, "Generative Grammar and Foreign Language Teaching." Paper presented at the Tenth International Congress of Linguistics, Bucharest, 1967.

Dolan, Sister Mary Edward, "Effect of a Modified Linguistics Word Recognition Program on Fourth-Grade Reading Achievement," *Reading Research Quarterly*, 1:4 (1966), 37-66.

Downing, John, "The Development of Linguistic Concepts in Children's Thinking," *Research in the Teaching of English*, 4 (1970), 5-19.

Downing, John, Daphne Cartwright, Barbara Jones, and William Latham, "Methodological Problems in the British i. t. a. Research," *Reading Research Quarterly*, 3:1 (1967), 85-99.

Durkin, Dolores, *Phonics and the Teaching of Reading*. 2nd ed. New York: Teachers College Press, 1965.

Edfeldt, Ake W., *Silent Speech and Silent Reading*. Chicago: University of Chicago Press, 1960.

Elkonin, D. B., *The Development of Speech in Preschool Age*. Moscow, 1958.

Emans, Robert, "The Usefulness of Phonic Generalizations above the Primary Grades," *Reading Teacher*, 20 (1967), 419-25.

Ervin, Susan M., "Imitation and the Structural Change in Children's Language," in *New Directions in the Study of Language*, Eric H. Lenneberg, ed. Cambridge: M. I. T. Press, 1964.

Ervin-Tripp, Susan M. and Dan I. Slobin, "Psycholinguistics," *Annual Review of Psychology*, 17 (1966), 435-74.

Fasold, Ralph W. and Walt Wolfram, "Some Linguistic Features of Negro Dialect," in *Teaching Standard English in the Inner City*, Ralph W. Fasold and Roger W. Shuy, eds. Washington: Center for Applied Linguistics, 1970.

Feldman, C. F. and M. Rodgon, "The Effects of Various Types of Adult Responses in the Syntactic Acquisition of Two- to Three-Year Olds." Unpublished paper, Department of Psychology, University of Chicago, 1970.

Fidelia, Sister Mary, "The Relative Effectiveness of Bloomfield's Linguistic Approach to Word Attack as Compared with *Phonics We Use*." Unpublished doctoral dissertation, University of Ottawa, 1959.

Fillmore, Charles J., "The Case for Case," in *Universals in Linguistic Theory*, E. Bach and R. T. Harms, eds. New York: Holt, Rinehart and Winston, 1968.

Fodor, Jerry A., "How to Learn to Talk: Some Simple Ways," in *The Genesis of Language: A Psycholinguistic Approach*, Frank Smith and George A. Miller, eds. Cambridge: M. I. T. Press, 1966.

Francis, W. Nelson, *The Structure of American English*. New York: Ronald Press, 1958.

Fries, Charles C., *Linguistics and Reading*. New York: Holt, Rinehart and Winston, 1963.

Fries, Charles C., *Teaching and Learning English as a Foreign Language*. Ann Arbor: University of Michigan Press, 1945.

Fries, Charles C., *The Structure of English*. New York: Harcourt, Brace & World, 1952.

Fries, Charles C., Agnes C. Fries, Rosemary G. Wilson, and Mildred K. Rudolph, *Merrill Linguistic Readers, Reader 1*. Columbus: Charles E. Merrill Books, 1966.

Fry, Edward B., "Comparing the Diacritical Marking System, i. t. a., and a Basal Reading Series," *Elementary English*, 43 (1966), 607-11.

Fry, Edward B., "i/ t/ a/: A Look at the Research Data," *Education*, 87 (1967), 549-53.

Gans, Roma, *Fact and Fiction about Phonics*. Indianapolis: Bobbs-Merrill, 1964.

Garrett, Michael and Jerry A. Fodor, "Psychological Theories and Linguistic Constructs," in *Verbal Behavior and General Behavior Theory*, T. R. Dixon and D. L. Horton, eds. Englewood Cliffs: Prentice-Hall, 1968.

Gleason, H. A., *An Introduction to Descriptive Linguistics*. Revised ed. New York: Holt, Rinehart and Winston, 1961.

Goffman, Erving, *Relations in Public*. New York: Basic Books, 1971.

Goodman, Kenneth S., "Reading: A Psycholinguistic Guessing Game," *Journal of the Reading Specialist*, 4 (1967), 126-35.

Hall, Robert A., *Introductory Linguistics*. Philadelphia: Chilton Company, 1964.

Hannerz, Ulf, *Soulside: Inquiries into Ghetto Culture and Community*. New York: Columbia University Press, 1969.

Harrell, L. E., "An Inter-Comparison of the Quality and Rate of the Development of the Oral and Written Language in Children," *Monographs of the Society for Research in Child Development*, No. 22, 1957.

Hauptman, Philip, "An Experimental Comparison of a Structural Approach and a Situational Approach to Foreign-Language Teaching." Unpublished doctoral dissertation, University of Michigan, 1970.

Hawkins, P. R., "Social Class, the Nominal Group and Reference," *Language and Speech*, 2 (1969), 125-35.

Hayes, Alfred S., Foreword to *Trends in Language Teaching*, Albert Valdman, ed New York: McGraw-Hill, 1966.

Heilman, Arthur W., *Phonics in Proper Perspective*. Columbus: Charles E. Merrill, 1964.

Hildreth, Gertrude, *Teaching Spelling*. New York: Henry Holt and Company, 1955.

Hill, Archibald A., *Introduction to Linguistic Structures*. New York: Harcourt, Brace & World, 1958.

Hockett, Charles F., *A Manual of Phonology*. Baltimore: Waverly Press, 1955.

Hockett, Charles F., *A Course in Modern Linguistics*. New York: Macmillan, 1958.

Hockett, Charles F. "Review of Eric H. Lenneberg's *Biological Foundations of Language*," *Scientific American*, 217:5 (1967), 141-44.

Jacobs, Rodney A. and Peter S. Rosenbaum, *English Transformational Grammar*. Waltham: Blaisdell, 1968.

Jenkins, J. and D. Palermo, "Mediation Processes and the Acquisition of Linguistic Structure," in *The Acquisition of Language*, Ursula Bellugi and Roger Brown, eds. *Monographs of the Society for Research in Child Development*, 29 (1964), Serial 92.

Jespersen, Otto, *Essentials of English Grammar*. London: George Allen & Unwin, 1933.

Jones, Daniel, *An Outline of English Phonetics*. Revised 8th ed. Cambridge: Heffer and Sons, 1957.

Kelley, K. L., *Early Syntactic Acquisition*. Santa Monica: Rand Corporation, 1967.

Kessel, F. S., "The Role of Syntax in Children's Comprehension from Ages Six to Twelve," *Monographs of the Society for Research in Child Development*, 6 (1970), Serial 139.

Klima, Edward S. and Ursula Bellugi, "Syntactic Regularities in the Speech of Children," in *Psycholinguistic Papers*, J. Lyons and R. Wales, eds. Edinburgh: Edinburgh University Press, 1966.

Krohn, Robert K., *English Sentence Structure*. Ann Arbor: University of Michigan Press, 1971.

Kuhn, Thomas S., *The Structure of Scientific Revolutions*. Chicago: University of Chicago Press, 1962.

Labov, William, *The Study of Nonstandard English*. Champaign: National Council of Teachers of English, 1970.

Labov, William, "Methodology," in *A Survey of Linguistic Science*, W. O. Dingwall, ed. College Park: University of Maryland, 1971.

Lado, Robert, *Linguistics Across Cultures*. Ann Arbor: University of Michigan Press, 1957.

Lado, Robert, *Language Teaching, A Scientific Approach*. New York: McGraw-Hill, 1964.

Lakoff, Robin, "Tense and its Relation to Participants," *Language*, 46:4 (1970), 838-49.

Langendoen, D. Terence, *Essentials of English Grammar*. New York: Holt, Rinehart and Winston, 1970.

Lawrence, Mary, *Writing as a Thinking Process*. Ann Arbor: University of Michigan Press, 1972.

Lefevre, Carl A., *Linguistics and the Teaching of Reading*. New York: McGraw-Hill, 1964.

Lenneberg, Eric H., "Understanding Language Without the Ability to Speak: A Case Report," *Journal of Abnormal Social Psychology*, 65 (1962), 419-25.

Lenneberg, Eric H., *Biological Foundations of Language*. New York: Wiley, 1967.

Lenneberg, Eric H., I. A. Nichols, and E. F. Rosenberger, "Primitive Stages of Language Development in Mongolism," *Proceedings of the Association for Research on Nervous and Mental Disease*, 42 (1964), 119-37.

Lenneberg, Eric H., F. G. Rebelsky, and I. A. Nichols, "The Vocalization of Infants Born to Deaf and to Hearing Parents," *Vita Humana*, 8 (1965), 23-37.

Lim, Kiat-Boey, "Prompting Versus Confirmation, Pictures Versus Translations." Unpublished doctoral dissertation, Harvard University, 1968.

Loban, Walter D., *The Language of Elementary School Children*. Champaign: National Council of Teachers of English, 1963.

Mackey, William F., *Language Teaching Analysis*. London: Longmans, 1965.

Malone, John R., "The Larger Aspects of Spelling Reform," *Elementary English*, 39 (1962), 435-45.

Marchand, Hans, *The Categories and Types of Present-Day English Word-Formation*. 2nd ed. Munich: C. H. Beck, 1969.

Marks, Lawrence E., "Some Structural and Sequential Factors in the Processing of Sentences," *Journal of Verbal Learning and Verbal Behavior*, 6 (1967), 707-13.

Mathews, Mitford H., *Teaching to Read: Historically Considered*. Chicago: University of Chicago Press, 1966.

Mazurkiewicz, Albert J., "Teaching Reading in America Using the Initial Teaching Alphabet," *Elementary English*, 41 (1964), 766-72.

Mazurkiewicz, Albert J., "A Comparison of i/ t/ a and t. o. Reading Achievement when Methodology is Controlled," *Elementary English* 43, (1966), 601-06, 69.

McCarthy, Dorothea, "Language Development in Children," in *Manual of Child Psychology*, Leonard Carmichael, ed. New York: Wiley, 1954.

McCawley, James D., "The Role of Semantics in a Grammar," in *Universals in Linguistic Theory*, E. Bach and R. T. Harms, eds. New York: Holt, Rinehart and Winston, 1968.

McKinnon, K. R., "An Experimental Study of the Learning of Syntax in Second Language Teaching." Unpublished doctoral dissertation, Harvard University, 1965.

McNeill, David, "Developmental Psycholinguistics," in *The Genesis of Language: A Psycholinguistic Approach*, Frank Smith and George A. Miller, eds. Cambridge: M. I. T. Press, 1966.

McNeill, David, "On the Theories of Language Acquisition," in *Verbal Behavior and General Behavior Theory*, T. R. Dixon and D. L. Horton, eds. Englewood Cliffs: Prentice-Hall, 1968.

McNeill, David, *The Acquisition of Language: The Study of Developmental Psycholinguistics*. New York: Harper & Row, 1970a.

McNeill, David, "The Development of Language," in *Carmichael's Manual of Child Psychology*, P. A. Mussen, ed. New York: Wiley, 1970b.

Mehler, Jacques and Peter Carey, "Role of Surface and Base Structure in the Perception of Sentences," *Journal of Verbal Learning and Verbal Behavior*, 6 (1967), 335-38.

Meltzer, N. S. and R. Herse, "The Boundaries of Written Words as seen by First Graders," *Journal of Reading Behavior*, 1 (1969), 3-13.

Menyuk, Paula, "A Preliminary Evaluation of Grammatical Capacity in Children," *Journal of Verbal Learning and Verbal Behavior*, 2 (1963a), 429-39.

Menyuk, Paula, "Syntactic Structures in the Language of Children," *Child Development*, 34 (1963b), 407-22.

Menyuk, Paula, *Sentences Children Use*. Cambridge: M. I. T. Press, 1969.

Miller, Wick and Susan M. Ervin, "The Development of Grammar in Child Language," in *The Acquisition of Language*, Ursula Bellugi and Roger Brown, eds. *Monographs of the Society for Research in Child Development*, 29 (1964), Serial 92.

Morley, Joan, *Improving Aural Comprehension*. Ann Arbor: University of Michigan Press, 1972.

Natchez, G. "From Talking to Reading Without Really Trying." *Reading Teacher*, 20 (1967), 339-42.

Newmark, Leonard and David A. Reibel, "Necessity and Sufficiency in Language Learning," *IRAL*, 6 (1969), 145-61.

O'Donnell, R. C., W. J. Griffin, and R. C. Norris, *Syntax of Kindergarten and Elementary School Children: A Transformational Analysis*. Champaign: National Council of Teachers of English, 1967.

Pike, Kenneth L., *Phonetics*. Ann Arbor: University of Michigan Press, 1943.

Politzer, Robert L., "An Investigation of the Order of Presentation of Foreign Language Grammar Drills in Relation to their Explanation," Office of Education Project 5-1096, 1967.

Reid, J. F., "Learning to Think about Reading," *Educational Research*, 9 (1966), 56-62.

Ritchie, William C., "Some Implications of Generative Grammar for the Construction of Courses in English as a Foreign Language," *Language Learning*, 17 (1967), 45-69, 111-31.

Ritchie, William C., "On the Explanation of Phonic Interference," *Language Learning*, 18 (1968), 183-97.

Rivers, Wilga, *The Psychologist and the Foreign Language Teacher*. Chicago: University of Chicago Press, 1964.

Ruddell, Robert B., "The Effect of the Similarity of Oral and Written Patterns of Language Structure on Reading Comprehension," *Elementary English*, 42 (1965), 403-10.

Ruddell, Robert B., "Reading Instruction in First Grade with Varying Emphasis on the Regularity of Grapheme-Phoneme Correspondences and the Relation of Language Structure to Meaning," *Reading Teacher*, 19 (1966), 653-60.

Russell, D. H. and Gretchen Wulfing, *The Ginn Basic Readers: Manual for Teaching the Third Reader - 2*. Revised ed. Boston: Ginn, 1955.

Rutherford, William, *Modern English*. New York: Harcourt, Brace and World, 1968.

Sachs, J., "The Status of Developmental Studies in Language," in *Human Development and Cognitive Processes*, J. Eliot, ed. New York: Holt, Rinehart and Winston, 1971.

Schane, Sanford A., *French Phonology and Morphology*. Cambridge: M. I. T. Press, 1968.

Scherer, George A. and Michael Wertheimer, *A Psycholinguistic Experiment in Foreign-Language Teaching*. New York: McGraw-Hill, 1964.

Schlesinger, I. M., "Production of Utterance and Language Acquisition," in *The Ontogenesis of Grammar: Facts and Theories*, Dan I. Slobin, ed. New York: Academic Press, 1971.

Schneyer, J. Wesley, " Reading Achievement of First Grade Children Taught by a Linguistic Approach and a Basal Reader Approach—Extended into Second Grade," *Reading Teacher* 20 (1967), 704-10.

Sheldon, William D. and Donald R. Lashinger, "Effects of First Grade Instruction Using Basal Readers, Modified Linguistic Materials, and Linguistic Readers," *Reading Teacher*, 19 (1966), 576-79.

Sinclair-de-Zwart, H., "Sensorimotor Action Schemes as a Condition of the Acquisition of Syntax." Unpublished paper, University of Geneva, 1968.

Sledd, James, "Double Speak: Dialectology in the Service of Big Brother," *College English*, 33: 4 (1972), 439-56.

Slobin, Dan I., "The Acquisition of Russian as a Native Language," in *The Genesis of Language: A Psycholinguistic Approach*, Frank Smith and George A. Miller, eds. Cambridge: M. I. T. Press, 1966a.

Slobin, Dan I., "Comments on 'Developmental Psycholinguistics'," in *The Genesis of Language: A Psycholinguistic Approach*, Frank Smith and George A. Miller, eds. Cambridge: M. I. T. Press, 1966b.

Slobin, D. I., "Imitation and Grammatical Development," in *Contemporary Issues in Developmental Psychology*, N. S. Endler, L. R. Boulter, and H. Osser, eds. New York: Holt, Rinehart and Winston, 1968.

Slobin, Dan I., "Early Grammatical Development in Several Languages with Special Attention to Soviet Research," in *The Structure and Psychology of Language*, Thomas G. Bever and W. Weksel, eds. New York: Holt, Rinehart and Winston, 1970a.

Slobin, Dan I., "Universals of Grammatical Development in Children," in *Advances in Psycholinguistics*, G. B. Flores d'Arcais and W. J. M. Levelt, eds. Amsterdam: North Holland Publishing Company, 1970b.

Slobin, Dan I., *Psycholinguistics*. Glenview: Scott, Foresman, 1971.

Slobin, Dan I. and C. A. Welsh, "Elicited Imitation as a Research Tool in Developmental Psycholinguistics." Unpublished paper, Department of Psychology, University of California, Berkeley, 1967.

Smith, Henry Lee, "Review of *Let's Read*," *Language*, 39 (1963), 67-78.

Southgate, Vera, "Approaching i. t. a. Results with Caution," *Reading Research Quarterly*, 1:3 (1966), 35-56.

Staats, Arthur W., *Language, Learning, and Cognition*. New York: Holt, Rinehart and Winston, 1968.

Staats, Arthur W. and Carolyn K. Staats, "A Comparison of the Development of Speech and Reading Behavior with Implications for Research," *Child Development*, 33 (1962), 831-46.

Staats, Arthur W. and Carolyn K. Staats, *Complex Human Behavior: A Systematic Extension of Learning Principles*. New York: Holt, Rinehart and Winston, 1963.

Stetson, R. H., *Motor Phonetics*. 2nd ed. Amsterdam: North Holland Publishing Company, 1951.

Stewart, William A., "Sociolinguistic Factors in the History of American Negro Dialects," *The Florida FL Reporter*, 5:2 (1967), 11,22,24,26.

Stewart, William A., "Continuity and Change in American Negro Dialects," *The Florida FL Reporter*, 6:1 (1968), 3-4, 14-16, 18.

Stewart, William A., "On the Use of Negro Dialect in the Teaching of Reading," in *Teaching Black Children to Read*, Joan C. Baratz and Roger W. Shuy, eds. Washington: Center for Applied Linguistics, 1969.

Stockwell, Robert P. and J. Donald Bowen, *The Sounds of English and Spanish*. Chicago: University of Chicago Press, 1965.

Stockwell, Robert P., J. Donald Bowen, and John W. Martin, *The Grammatical Structures of English and Spanish*. Chicago: University of Chicago Press, 1965.

Strickland, Ruth G., "The Language of Elementary School Children: Its Relationship to the Language of Reading Textbooks and the Quality of Reading of Selected Children," *Bulletin of the School of Education*, Indiana University, 38, 1962.

Thomas, Owen, *Tranformational Grammar and The Teachers of English*. New York: Holt, Rinehart and Winston, 1965.

Trager, George L. and Henry Lee Smith, *An Outline of English Structure*. Norman: Studies in Linguistics, Occasional Papers, 3, 1951.

Valdman, Albert, ed., *Trends in Language Teaching*. New York: McGraw-Hill, 1966.

Venezky, Richard L., "English Orthography: Its Graphical Structure and its Relation to Sound," *Reading Research Quarterly*, 2:3 (1967), 75-105.

Vygotsky, L. S., *Thought and Language*. Cambridge: M. I. T. Press, 1962.

Wardhaugh, Ronald, "Linguistic Insights into the Reading Process," *Language Learning*, 18 (1968), 235-52.

Wardhaugh, Ronald, *Reading: A Linguistic Perspective*. New York: Harcourt, Brace and World, 1969.

Wardhaugh, Ronald, *Introduction to Linguistics*. New York: McGraw-Hill, 1972.

Watson, James D., *The Double Helix*. London: Weidenfeld & Nicolson, 1968.

Weaver, Wendell W., "The Word as the Unit of Language," *Journal of Reading*, 10 (1967), 262-68,

Weaver, Wendell W. and Albert J. Kingston, "Psychological Examinations of Newer Dimensions of Linguistics and their Implications for Reading," *Journal of Reading*, 11 (1967), 238-42.

Weir, Ruth, *Language in the Crib*. The Hague: Mouton, 1962.

Weksel, W., "Review of Ursula Bellugi and Roger Brown, eds. *The Acquisition of Language*," *Language*, 41 (1965), 692-709.

Wijk, Axel, *Rules of Pronunciation for the English Language*. London: Oxford University Press, 1966.

Wilson, G., ed., *A Linguistic Reader*. New York: Harper & Row, 1967.

Wilson, Rosemary G. and Helen G. Lindsay, "Applying Linguistics to Remedial Reading," *Reading Teacher*, 16 (1963), 452-55,

Wohleber, Sister Mary, "A Study of the Effects of a Systematic Program of Phonetic Training on Reading Instruction." Unpublished doctoral dissertation, University of Pittsburgh, 1953.

Wolfe, David L., "Some Theoretical Aspects of Language Learning and Language Teaching," *Language Learning*, 17 (1967), 173-88.